The Mauve Decade

The
Mauve Decade

---

*American Life at the End
of the Nineteenth Century*

THOMAS BEER

CARROLL & GRAF PUBLISHERS, INC.
NEW YORK

First Carroll & Graf edition 1997

Carroll & Graf Publishers, Inc.
19 West 21st Street
New York, NY 10010-6805

Library of Congress Cataloging-in-Publication Data
  Beer, Thomas, 1889–1940.
      The mauve decade : American life at the end of the nineteenth
  century / Thomas Beer. — 1st Carroll & Graf ed.
        p.   cm.
      Originally published: New York : A. A. Knopf. 1926.
      ISBN 0-7867-0501-9
      1. American literature—19th century—History and criticism.   2.
  United States—Social life and customs—19th century.   3. National
  characteristics, American, in literature.   4. United States—
  Intellectual life—1865–1918.   5. United States—Civilization—
  1865–1918.   I. Title.
  PS214.B35   1997
  810.9'004—dc21   97-17485
                                                            CIP

Manufactured in the United States of America

PREFACE
ADDRESSED TO READERS
BORN AFTER 1900 A.D.

Alcott, Amos Bronson (*1799–1888*). *Born at Walcott, Conn. Peddler, schoolmaster, lecturer, practicing philosopher. Established a communist colony for farming in Harvard township, 1843. Subsequently dean of the Concord school of philosophy. Principal works: Orphic Sayings, Tablets, Ralph Waldo Emerson: His Character and Genius.*

Alcott, Louisa May (*1832–1888*). *Born in Germantown, Pa. Educated at random. Began literary hackwork in 1855. Health impaired by illness contracted while nursing soldiers at Georgetown in 1862–3. Principal works: Hospital and Campfire Sketches, Moods, Little Women, Little Men, An Old Fashioned Girl, Eight Cousins, Rose in Bloom, Jo's Boys, Jack and Jill and Under the Lilacs.*

Alden, Henry Mills (*1836–1919*). *Born at Mount Tabor, Vt. Educated for the ministry. Attracted attention through studies in Hellenic culture. Editorially connected with Harper's Magazine and Harper's Weekly for forty years. His volumes of metaphysic, God in His World, and, A Study of Death, are similar in theory to ideas of Henri Bergson.*

Aldrich, Thomas Bailey (*1836–1907*). *Born at Portsmouth, N. H. His light verse and compressed,*

7

graceful tales made him popular in the '70s. He inherited The Atlantic Monthly's editorship from William Dean Howells in 1881 and held it until 1890. His importance was largely that of remarkable personal charm, although he sometimes produced pleasing effects in verse. Principal works: The Story of a Bad Boy, Marjorie Daw, Mercedes and Later Lyrics, Judith of Bethulia.

Allen, Charles Grant Blairfindie *(1848–1899). Born at Kingston, Canada. Began to write as an undergraduate at Merton College, Oxford. Taught school in Jamaica and returned to London. He lectured extensively and wrote numbers of brilliant critical essays, uncollected, showing a considerable bent for psychology. Principal works: Physiological Aesthetics, The Color Sense, Philistia, The Woman Who Did, Hilda Wade, The Evolution of the Idea of God and a translation of The Attis of Catullus.*

Bierce, Ambrose *(1842– ?). Born in Meigs County, Ohio. He served with gallantry in the Civil War, and was severely wounded. Even his earliest humorous sketches were grim. He was a journalist and editor in California until 1895, when he came to the East. His work was not unappreciated but, in spite of its genuine distinction, it was unpopular owing to a monotonous insistence on death and fantastic calamity. Bierce vanished in Mexico in 1916 and his end is unknown. Principal works: In the Midst of Life, Black Beetles in Amber, The Devil's Dictionary, The Monk and the Hangman's Daughter.*

Burton, Sir Richard *(1821–1890). He was largely educated in Europe and acquired an amazing dextrous-*

ness in Oriental languages during his early life in India and Africa. His reputation was established by a pilgrimage in disguise to Medina and Mecca in 1852. He translated The Arabian Nights, without expurgation, as well as Il Pentamerone and the poems of Camoens. His other translations, books of travel and essays in geography make up twenty volumes.

Carryl, Guy Wetmore *(1872–1903). Born in New York. His cynical, light verse stamped him as a humorist and in Zut he used the artificial forms of Robert Louis Stevenson, but his last work, The Lieutenant Governor, showed a drift into realism and satire.*

Cope, Edward Drinker *(1840–1897). Born at Philadelphia of a distinguished Quaker family. His aptitude for natural science appeared when he was a child and at sixteen he was already writing notes, in Quaker dialect, on fossils. He spent his life in zoology and paleontology and in exploring the west for specimens. His scientific writings and discussions are too candidly free of popular values to be read by people without an education in the subject, but his influence was tremendous both in Europe and America. He cooperated with Josiah Willard Gibbs, the American authority on thermodynamics and statistical mechanics, in forwarding the Society for the Advancement of Science. His name appears upward of five thousand times in the proceedings of European and English scientific bodies.*

Davis, Rebecca Harding *(1831–1910). Born at Washington, Pa. She achieved an almost scandalous fame in 1861 by the publication of Life in the Iron Mills and Margaret Howth, both social studies of unusual frankness. Her temperament was realistic and her feminism took the highly practical bent of demanding respectable wages and vocational freedom for women. Her later fiction is of no great interest but her essays on celebrities and localities were amusing and vigorous to the last.*

Du Chaillu, Paul Belloni *(1835–1903). Born in New Orleans but removed to France as a child. His first accounts of explorations in equatorial Africa were received with open derision as fabulous and for years he was involved in arguments and assertions until subsequent explorers righted him with the public. He became interested in Scandinavia and produced an excellent text on its primitive civilizations. In his later life he resided considerably in New York. He is best represented by* The Gorilla Country, Explorations and Adventures in Equatorial Africa *and* The Viking Age.

Ford, Paul Leicester *(1865–1902). Born in Brooklyn. He was privately educated and widely travelled before he became interested in historiography. He edited the writings of Thomas Jefferson, explored Americana of the eighteenth century, wrote sketches of Washington and Franklin which show the tide of American historical writing on the turn from sentimental bombast to research and sanity. His fiction is generally banal, although* The Honorable Peter Stirling *is amusing as a description of a heavy politician. Mr. Ford busied himself in calling attention to the wretched preservation of documents and records in the United States and established a magazine of bibliography shortly before he was brutally murdered by his brother in 1902.*

George, Henry *(1839–1897). Born at Philadelphia.*

After a roving boyhood he appeared as a radical journalist in San Francisco. The publication, in 1879, of Progress and Poverty made him famous. His advocacy of the single tax—i. e., the reduction of real estate to common property by the imposition of a tax equal to the total rental value of the land, aroused horror and admiration. He was even denounced by the Duke of Argyll. In 1886 he was a contestant for the mayoralty of New York City in a political turmoil accelerated by the priest, Edward MacGlynn, who denounced Catholic interference with American affairs. Mr. George was defeated by the combined forces of conservatives and Catholics. He died in 1897 while candidate a second time for the mayoralty of New York.

Godkin, Edwin Lawrence *(1831–1902). Born at Moyne, Ireland. He came to the United States in 1856. In 1881 his review, The Nation, became a weekly issue of The New York Evening Post, Godkin assuming the editorship of both the newspaper and the magazine. His editorials indubitably influenced public thought in the United States and aided in the renovation of the Democratic Party in 1884. For a competent characterization see, Some Newspapers and Newspapermen by Oswald Villard, as Mr. Godkin's official biography is an atrocity.*

Huntington, Collis Potter *(1821–1900). Born at Harwinton, Conn. At the age of sixteen he became a clock peddler and did very well. In 1849 he transferred his abilities to California. In 1860 he, with Charles Crocker, Leland Stanford and Mark Hopkins, conceived the transcontinental railway and in 1869 the Central Pacific was finished, at the expense of a number of people* *and states. This line was absorbed in the Southern Pacific Railroad, of which Mr. Huntington was the controlling power. His character was constantly attacked, and when the Southern Pacific attempted to excuse itself from the debts of the Central Pacific, the financier became an object of malignant insinuations. But he built a church in his native town to the memory of his mother, donated extensively to Hampton Institute in Virginia, gave $50,000 to Tuskegee Institute in Alabama and expressed his benevolence in countless ways, so that his aid was sought by representatives of the most respected organizations for the promotion of human well-being and of reform.*

Norris, Frank *(1870–1902). Born at Chicago. He studied in Paris and at Harvard. His first important novel, Vandover and the Brute, could not be published until after his death. He edited The Wave at San Francisco, reported the Cuban campaign and then lived in New York for a short period. There is no biography of this artist. His principal works are: McTeague, Blix, The Octopus and The Pit.*

CONTENTS

THE TITANESS

1

THEY laid Jesse James in his grave and Dante Gabriel Rossetti died immediately. Then Charles Darwin was deplored and then, on April 27, 1882, Louisa May Alcott hurried to write in her journal: "Mr. Emerson died at 9 P. M. suddenly. Our best and greatest American gone. The nearest and dearest friend Father has ever had and the man who helped me most by his life, his books and his society. Illustrious and beloved friend, good-bye!" So she made a lyre of yellow jonquils for Ralph Waldo Emerson's preposterous funeral and somehow steered Bronson Alcott through the dreary business until he stood beside the coffin in the damp cemetery and mechanically drawled out the lines of a dire poem. Under the shock the tall old idler was a mere automaton with a bloodless face that startled watchers as he stepped back from the grave into which his one importance sank. Emerson was going from him! He was losing his apologist, his topic. His fingers fell on the shoulder of a little boy who had pressed forward to see and the grip became so cruel that Louisa saw and her hoarse voice rose in the hush, commanding: "Pa! Let go! You're hurting Georgie's arm!" But her father could hear nothing. She stooped and wrenched the child's arm free.

All summer long, Bronson Alcott paced through Concord's placid loveliness, being Bronson Alcott still, still ready to let flow the wondrous volume of his stored inanity on any victim. But ghosts may have stalked with him beneath the royal elms, for when his school of limp philosophers gathered in July, he said to Frances Hedges: "I am the last. They are all gone but me." And they were gone—Hawthorne, Thoreau, the obsessed Sumner and the bloody Theodore Parker; and now Emerson had left him. True, Holmes survived, and so did Lowell. But they had never been too friendly, and neither was young Howells a great admirer, nor that dapper, handsome poet, much too suave—his name was Aldrich—who once so upset a session of the Radical Club by reciting some satirical verses about an improper woman in a harem.

> "Then, at a wave of her sunny hand,
> The dancing girls of Samarcand
> Float in like mists of Fairyland!
> And to the low voluptuous swoons
> Of music rise and fall the moons
> Of their full brown bosoms. . . .
> And there in this Eastern paradise
> Filled with the fumes of sandalwood,
> And Khoten musk and aloes and myrrh,
> Sits Rose in Bloom on a silk divan,
> Sipping the wines of Astrakhan,
> And her Arab lover sits with her. . . ."

No, Bronson Alcott was wasted on this new society of fribbles and light poets in which men applauded the ribaldries of Mark Twain, whose flippancy Louisa had reproved in her "Eight Cousins," in which the Radical

Club was forgotten. His occupation and his audience ceased beside Emerson's flowery casket. Emerson had approved him in all his stages—Platonist schoolmaster, vegetarian, communist, transcendentalist, abolitionist. Bronson Alcott had repaid the devotion with devotion. A new phrase of his Emerson roused in the shallow pond of his intelligence the noisy splash of a log rolled down some slope into a tepid flood. As he lounged from hotel to hotel in summers, he spoke of Emerson as warmly as he spoke of Duty or Domestic Loyalty or Purity or Unselfishness. For Alcott was not an ungrateful man, although an idealist by profession and practice. Idealism is best supported on an income and, after the death of his proud wife's father, Alcott had no banker.

He somehow married the daughter of Samuel May, a rather leonine lady, kin to the Sewalls and Frothinghams. She refused food when her husband's idiotic communist farm at Harvard failed, perhaps from sheer exhaustion, as she had toiled in the fields with her impubic children while Alcott, clad in white linen, talked to callers and explained his high purposes to Margaret Fuller under shady trees. Emerson rescued the family. Emerson brooded affectionately over the growing girls while Mrs. Alcott had an employment office in Boston, on behalf of Alcott's inexhaustible idealism. The older daughters wore frocks bestowed by cousins and an aunt. Louisa went out as a maid once, and once contemplated marriage with a wealthy unloved suitor and once considered suicide. She taught school; she wrote trash for newspapers; she ran errands. Alcott addressed her as "duty's faithful child" in one of his insufferable poems and rhetorically clasped her to his bosom in recognition of her merits, which, he wrote to a friend, gave him every satisfaction. It seems fair. Her first, forgotten novel "Moods" had just made a stir, even causing Henry James, Junior—"a very literary youth," says Louisa's journal—to commit an act of enthusiasm in print. But "Moods" did not sell and Emerson's benevolence continued. It appears that he found for Alcott a paying post in the hospital service at Washington when war broke out, but he was obliged to tell the offering powers that Mr. Alcott had "other projects," which consisted, as far as there is record, in a hearty admiration of the Bostonian excitement over a situation highly profitable to Boston, together with some occasional speeches for the holy cause.

Louisa went to nursing in the hospitals and Alcott quite closely approached the rim of slaughter when he had to bring her home in icy trains, delirious with typhoid and pneumonia, all the way from Washington to Concord. What Louisa thought of his notions about tending a sick daughter we shall never know, as she destroyed much of her journal in the autumn of 1887 when she was so wrecked that she took refuge with Dr. Rhoda Lawrence and sat making penwipers of flannel in the shape of carnations, waiting for death at the age of fifty-four. But the experience gave her material for "Hospital and Campfire Sketches." She became popular, and money oozed on the arid contours of Alcott's massive debts. Then her publisher wanted a book for girls. She didn't much like girls. Girls, it is possible, had always been rather shy of the Alcott

sisters with their bad gowns and their curious papa.
But she could write of herself and her family, so she
wrote that first part of "Little Women"—and there it
is, simple and as effortless as though she had spilled
bright rags of silk from her lap on sunlit grass beneath
a blowing lilac-tree.

Louisa May Alcott was famous. Her bones ached;
her voice had become hoarse and coarse; doctors gave her
opiates and treatments that would scare a modern physician badly; she had no use for popularity and no taste
for the world that now blandished before her. Pleasure? A trip to Europe with her youngest sister, May.
She must nurse her mother and pay Pa's debts and make
sure of the family's future. Alcott went beaming and
rosy in the very best broadcloth and linen to lecture on
Duty, Idealism and Emerson before larger audiences,
which now looked eagerly at the grandfather of "Little
Women." Duty's child was hard at work, writing
"moral pap for the young," in her own phrase, and
paralysing a thumb by making three copies of a serial
at once. Once she walked across the lawns of Vassar
among the thronging girls who tore bits of lace from
her dull gown, shook hands with Maria Mitchell, the
astronomer, who privately held that Miss Alcott's books
were namby-pamby nonsense, but thought the tall
spinster a fine woman. And once at Syracuse she faced
a congress of her sex and heard its applause as women
wrung her fingers. She worked, and Alcott prattled
to and fro. Her mother slowly died after looking up
at Alcott with the singular remark, "You have laid
a very soft pillow for me to go to sleep on." And in

the summer of 1882 she worked still, arranging monstrous lunches and teas for the students of the Alcottian school of philosophy, scolding her adored, handsome nephews, permitting Miss Frances Hedges to help her with preserves and ginger cakes, and pausing between jobs to mend a coat or stitch a baseball for any lad who swung over the fence and came prowling around to the kitchen in search of Miss Lou. Men had no interest for Louisa, but a court of adolescents hummed about her to be lectured for sneaking off to Boston to see that awful French troupe in *La Grande Duchesse* and *La Belle Hélène*, and to be fed ginger cakes. Little Miss Hedges had come to be irradiated by the wisdom of Bronson Alcott, but she fell into subjection before Alcott's daughters and wrote to her father in crude Illinois: "I just cannot see anything remarkable or interesting in Mr. Alcott at all, but it is a *privilege* to know Miss Alcott and Mrs. Pratt [the "Meg" of "Little Women"]. They had the awfullest time when they were girls. Sometimes they did not have enough to eat and I have met some ladies here who think that Mr. Alcott has always treated his family shamefully. . . ." Alcott would probably have been much astonished to know that anybody had such thoughts of him. There is an indurating quality in the practice of idealism. It is true that Louisa's journal contains notes of restlessness under the spell of duty. In April of 1877 she wrote: "I'm selfish. I want to go away and rest in Europe. Never shall," and in August of 1882 she sent word after Miss Hedges that she was going to take her favourite nephew, Johnny Pratt, out to Cali-

fornia and have "a good, long, selfish rest." Never did.
In September her father collapsed and thereafter lay
a prisoner in a pretty room lined with books, chattering
more and more feebly, but chattering still.

All this while the fat volumes of Louisa May Alcott
had gone swarming in ugly covers across America from
the press of Roberts Brothers, spreading the voice not of
Bronson Alcott but of Abba May, his wife, a Puritan
lady born in 1799. Her biographer admits that Louisa
was unfitted by nature to comprehend Bronson Alcott.
In the journal he is "my handsome old philosopher" but
it isn't evident that his child cared for transcendentalism.
In "Little Women," "Little Men" and "Jo's Boys," Pa
is the merest shadow, and the heroic males of the long
series are either handsome lads or brisk, successful bearded
doctors, men who would hardly lug a delirious lady
four hundred miles in railway coaches and who always
have cash in pocket. Such philosophy as the books
hold is just what Abba May had taught her children,
and when the young folk of the tales have flared into
a moment of wilful hedonism, it is a firm, kind lady,
middle-aged, who steps forward and puts them right.
Louisa was writing "moral pap." She couldn't conceive an unmoral book for children, and her own morality
hadn't shifted since it was pressed into her by Ma,
who had Louisa analyse her small self in a diary for
inspection. Pa's lessons, such as "Apollo eats no meat
and has no beard . . . " seem to have faded from
her completely. God's ministrant is always female,
sometimes abetted in virtue by one of the bearded
doctors, and always a success. The children wriggle for

a breath and then are towed meekly in the cool tide of rectitude. One learns a deal of Abba May Alcott in the progress. She was charmed with "Eight Cousins," in which her representative rebukes current books for boys, the nonsense of Horatio Alger and Oliver Optic, with a fleet slap for "Innocents Abroad," and comments:"It gives them such wrong ideas of life and business; shows them so much evil and vulgarity that they need not know about. . . . It does seem to me that someone should write stories that should be lively, natural and helpful—tales in which the English should be good, the morals pure and the characters such as we can love in spite of the faults that all may have. . . ." She must have been delighted with "Rose in Bloom," in which Rose Campbell gives talks on conduct to other girls in the dressing-rooms of balls, throws over her lover when he comes in a state of champagne to wish her a happy New Year, and waltzes only with her male cousins. She did not live to read "Jo's Boys," which decides that men who have been, no matter how forgivably, in prison may not woo pure young girls. Righteous diversion? A jolly picnic on the river or a set of patriotic tableaux; a romp on the sands at Nonquit; red apples and a plate of gingerbread after sledding in winters; tennis and rootbeer under the elms in summer.

It is a voice of that fading generation which crowned William Dean Howells and shuddered with pleasure as it dabbled its hands in strong Russian waters, for Miss Alcott found "Anna Karenina" most exciting and liked "Kings in Exile" with its pictures of a dissolute Europe. She would even recommend Le Père Goriot as suitable reading for a girl of eighteen, but as for "Huckleberry Finn," why, "if Mr. Clemens cannot think of something better to tell our pure-minded lads and lasses, he had best stop writing for them." . . . But she went on writing moral pap for the young and it sold prodigiously. The critics paid no particular attention. Miss Alcott wrote admirably for our little folk. It seems to have struck nobody that Miss Alcott's first audience, the girls who had wept over "Little Women" in the latter '60's were now rearing their daughters in an expanded world on the same diet. In 1882 Joseph Choate turned on a witness in one of his cross-examinations with the cry, "Good God, madame! Did you think that your husband was one of Miss Alcott's boys?" but the lawyer was a profane fellow, given to whist and long dinners. There was no discussion of Miss Alcott's morality, and certainly nobody talked of her art: she wrote for the young.

As spring of 1888 drew near, certain improvident small Bostonians in the region of Louisburg Square's marshalled prettiness were aware of a benevolent goddess whose dark carriage came daily to a rented house. If you ran quickly to open the door, you were sure of a hoarse joke and some pennies and, if you were a small male, a kiss and the loan of a laced handkerchief should your nose need wiping. The goddess, known by the rather Syriac title of "Msalkot," was in the form of a tall lady whose handsome body shivered constantly under furred wraps and whose brown hair showed no grey. Sometimes she came out of the house with a plate of some quivering dessert or a bunch of black foreign grapes untouched by the dotard upstairs in his hired shrine. Sometimes she came out weeping quietly on the arm of a grave nephew if Pa had not known her that day. Once she picked up little Patrick Keogh and held him against her weary barrenness all the way to Dunreath Place and gave him a bath in Rhoda Lawrence's tub. She had nothing left for herself. Her sister's sons were grown. Her will was made, asking that she be buried across the feet of her family, as she had always cared for them in life and would rest better so. On March 3rd some acute infant may have noted that the lady wore no furs. Chill wind pursued the carriage as she drove away. In the morning came the daze and agony of a new pain. She asked: "Is it not meningitis?" But at noon she could not know that Bronson Alcott had stopped talking, and before a second sunset duty's child went hurrying after him.

The journals observed that she had been an admirable writer for the young. Mayo Hazeltine stated casually that "Miss Alcott has found imitators among writers who aspired to something more than the entertainment of nurseries." The gentle, forgotten Constance Woolson exclaimed on paper: "How she has been imitated!" and resumed the imitation of Henry James, a habit in which she so far progressed that "A Transplanted Boy" might have been written and destroyed by James himself. It was plain, to be sure, that a cooing legion was now busy in devising tales on the Alcottian formula, and one follower, Margaret Sidney, was simply a vulgar duplicate of Miss Alcott. But the reviewers generally had little to say of an influence, loosed and active for

26

a quarter of a century, embedded in grown women from the nursery, familiar as a corset. Louisa May Alcott passed without judgment or summary. The critics faced thrilling importations just then and space must be kept for the discussion of "Robert Elsmere," an announcement by a Mrs. Humphry Ward that she had receded from strict belief in the divine origin of Jesus Christ, a fact somehow more exhilarating than the similar recession of her kinsman Matthew Arnold. And then there was "As in a Looking-Glass" with delicious illustrations by George Du Maurier, in whose pages one learned of a raffish woman who married a virtuous landholder and then poisoned herself when her past rose to be a nuisance. Its morality had to be discussed in long columns, just as the morality of its stepchild, "The Second Mrs. Tanqueray," would be discussed sixty months later. These foreign wares had natural precedence of the case of an American spinster, born of a dismoded philosopher, and full justice had been done when six notices mentioned that Louisa May Alcott was a type of the nation's pure and enlightened womanhood.

Even before the Civil War, orators had flung to the female margin of their audiences some variation of a phrase that always concluded with the trisyllabic word, "womanhood." Theodore Parker used "our pure and enlightened womanhood" four times in two years. Daniel Sickles produced "our world conquering and enlightened womanhood" a few days before he shot his wife's paramour in the streets of Washington. Roscoe Conkling sprinkled his speeches with references to "a pure, enlightened and progressive womanhood" and had

more than six hundred babies named for him, to say
nothing of one proved "Roscina Conkling" in Ohio.
Chester Arthur begot "our cultured and enlightened
womanhood" shortly after he startled a dinner in his
honour at Saratoga by remarking that he might be President of the United States but his private life was
nobody's damned business. Ulysses Grant was also
President, but he said nothing much about women and
was defended by his doctors and family in his last days
from committees of ladies and ancillary clergymen
demanding that he sign warnings against the use of
alcohol and tobacco. Robert Ingersoll spoke touchingly
of the nobility of womanhood quite often, and his version
of the tribute is identical with that used by Susan Brownell Anthony and Lucy Stone. There was some convention of the editorial desk and platform in favour of a
noble womanhood currently to be viewed in America,
and the phrase echoed broadly in 1889 when a yearning
for suffrage crystallized under the leadership of Elizabeth Cady Stanton. Miss Grace Ralston caught the
words from air about her and made use of "the nobility
of womanhood" to a courtly, charming gentleman in
a Bostonian drawing-room. "Just what," he asked the
girl, "is the nobility of womanhood?" Miss Ralston
was annoyed. She had in her possession a dried rose
once the property of Elizabeth Stanton and some letters
from Lucy Stone. The nobility of womanhood was . . .
why, it was the nobility of womanhood! The pleasant
gentleman seemed amazingly dull. What precisely was
the nobility of womanhood? Miss Ralston had to

lecture him stringently. The nobility of womanhood meant the nobility of womanhood! Anybody knew that! "Yes," said William James, "but just what is it, my dear?"

The year 1889 is stippled with unrecorded criticism of American womanhood, besides the printed observation of Rudyard Kipling who found it wasted time to call on the grand pirates of San Francisco in their homes as wives and daughters adopted the dark young man from India. The house belonged to the womenfolk and it was vain to hint that he had come to see its owner. In March Mlle. Suzanne Beret was appalled by the strangeness of Cleveland as she taught French in a wealthy family and wrote to a cousin in New York: "The ladies talk of nothing but adultery to each other, although they never tell amusing stories of love-affairs. . . . I do not accustom myself to the rudeness with which young girls treat men older than themselves. M. Eltinoit* made Miss X a compliment on her costume at a dinner last week by saying she resembled Sarah Bernhardt. She responded: 'Shut up! How dare you compare me to such a woman!' . . . They treat their sons and husbands as rudely before people as though they were bad servants. . . . They are much more loyal to each other than Frenchwomen would be. . . ." She could make nothing of such a situation. Home-sickness overcame her and she went back to Nantes and to matrimony. In June a Mrs. Edward Wharton of Boston gave offence to a matron from

* Elton Hoyt.

Chicago by remarking on the rudeness of American ladies to their sons, but was something forgiven on account of a lovely white parasol. In October the curious Grant Allen gave some advice to an English friend starting for New York and concluded: "Be careful about involving yourself in arguments with ladies. American women take offence easily. With them argument is not intellectual but always emotional and if you attack any little belief or vanity you will find that they can be very rude indeed." Allen knew countless Americans and was himself a Canadian. He later chose to refer rather coldly to "American girls indulged by 'poppa' and spoiled beyond endurance by 'mamma' who make life intolerable and ordinary conversation inaudible for a considerable distance around them," although, among his many avocations, he was a feminist and raised a storm with a feminist novel, "The Woman Who Did," in 1895. His whole literary course was unsteady and a perplexity to critics. He applauded good popular art as good popular art and found the low comedian, Dan Leno, more amusing than Sir Henry Irving. He wrote readable bits of botany, translated from Catullus, composed guide-books, and invented, in a story, a prelude to the psychological entertainments of Sigmund Freud. One comes to-day on his name in volumes of reminiscence or in dusty copies of the *Strand* with some surprise. . . . But, for all these dubious undertones, 1889 was a year of triumph for American womanhood. Without parade or notice, outside Chicago, a settlement for the poor was opened by Jane Addams and Ellen Starr in September with the name, "Hull House," and at Lake Forest, on

Christmas Day, Helen Kimball, a child of ten, was asked to define the word "author" and with the speed of true intelligence answered: "An author is a dreadful person who likes to write books." The last decade of the nineteenth century could now begin.

It began with a handsome exhortation from Phillips Brooks, who urged it to be a good decade. Susan Anthony wished it well, but symptoms of frivolity appeared too soon. In the West some young Indians imagined that they saw a Son of the Great Spirit walking the waters and their aboriginal fancy led them to represent this messenger as having nail-pierced hands and feet. The absurdity didn't prevent tribes from believing that a promise of a happier land teeming with buffalo had been made. So lone agents and commanders of outlying forts were alarmed by the Ghost Dance. Naked altogether or striped with paint and floating wolfskins, lads spun and trotted in monotonous rhythms. Some whisper ran down deserts into Mexico and there they danced with green feathers laced to ankles above feet that padded in the noise of drums. Old Sitting Bull now had callers at his shack. His attitude toward the paleface had always been tinged by a dour conservatism, and after Major Kossuth Elder translated to him Longfellow's awful poem on the death of Custer at the Little Big Horn he was heard to state a preference for Negroes. It is said that he was spider in a vast conspiracy, red and black, to drive the white man altogether from America but unhappily he was killed before his plans had time to mature. . . . In the East, too, dancing held the eye. Dandies packed Koster and Bial's profane hall nightly to applaud the stamp and flutter of Carmencita as the tall Spaniard whirled and swayed in smoky light. Ladies came veiled to inspect the prodigy and she outdid in gossip the fame of Richard Harding Davis or of Richard Mansfield, who returned to female favour in the "Beau Brummell" of a young playwright, Clyde Fitch. Carmencita's red and yellow gowns covered her legs entirely and her shoulders were hidden in sleeves. It is plain that she wore corsets and nothing lewd is recorded of her performances, in public, while in private she seems to have been an estimable, stupid creature, like most artists, but in October the peace of the *Sun's* office was invaded by five matrons from Chicago, headed by a Mrs. Walker, who demanded that Charles Dana suppress Carmencita forthwith. The editor was habitually deferential to women and notably patient in conversation with fools, but his cynical humour roused behind the kindly mask. He asked if the committee had seen the Spaniard dance. No, but she was an immoral person and the *Sun* must wither this ribald bloom straightway. Chicago then contained a dive of ferocious note among men, mentioned discreetly in journals when it vanished and since recalled in the documents of psychiatrists. Did the ladies not think that they should suppress "the Slide" before they began to rearrange New York? They had never heard of such a place. "Well," said Dana, "you go back to Chicago and have them shut the Slide, and then I'll have Carmencita run out of town for you." The committee bustled forth. . . . Carmencita danced and danced. In 1893 male tourists went secretly and timidly to behold the odd assemblies at the Slide when the World's Fair packed Chicago. But on April 7, 1891, Dana wrote to an old friend in Illinois: "I do not see why you cannot keep your lady reformers at home. They come in here so thick and fast that I am thinking of attaching a portcullis to my office just to keep them out. If I do not let them waste my time proposing some foolish amendment to the laws they insult me by mail, and if I do see them they insult me anyhow. If you hear of any more nuisances starting for the *Sun*, tell them to try Godkin at the *Post*."

2

America had already seen the two best criticisms of its civilization produced by European authority, and neither Matthew Arnold nor James Bryce had taken much heed to the problem, simple in England, of housekeeping in the United States. It was bad enough for women of the Eastern ports to find suitable servants. Civil War and Indian troubles had kept immigration scanty in the Middle West through the '70's and '80's. The Swedes and Germans arrived, to be sure, but either as tribes or as bachelors. Life in Chicago was made more difficult by "the servant question," and life among the moneyed in Omaha and Council Bluffs was nothing less than a twisted cozenage of Karens and Ludmillas, certain to betray a mistress for the gain of another weekly dollar and always likely to announce a sudden marriage with some dumb suitor just as invitations had been sent for an important dinner. In 1882 an heiress of Omaha saw for the first time in her twenty years a house in Chicago attended by four servants, and the primary renown of Mrs. Potter Palmer outside her windy realm along the Lake was that she kept six servants. The condition suppled and made practical young wives of the midland. They must be practical or perish, socially. Dinner had to be cooked and the clock from the Philadelphia Centennial had to be dusted. Rudyard Kipling briefly bade his friends in India be thankful for their cheap and biddable hirelings after he had dashed from side to side of the continent, seeing half of the situation. As early as 1880 there began to be talk of "the lure of the great cities" and bright in the golden phantasmagory of a house in New York or Chicago stood the shape of the Hired Girl. So when Grace had scolded or cajoled Olga in the kitchen toward some pallid comprehension of boiling jelly and had bestowed Robby in his red express cart under the maples of the front yard with a hope that Sue wasn't playing with those possibly lousy Swedish children around the corner, she fell wearily into the hammock with Mrs. Constance Cary Harrison's new novel and permitted the perfume of that metropolitan world to thrill her gently. A nurse-maid for the children was usually as fantastic a dream as the English governess of mundane fiction. She could read of shopping-trips along Twenty-third Street, but if she sketched one for herself, why, who would take care of Sue and Robby? Thus Fred, idling up the street at half past four, or driving in from an inspection of the farm outside town left to his namesake by Uncle Fred, might be met by a wistful suggestion about the "niceness" of living in New York or Chicago. Perhaps some second blooming of the Teutonic immigration took over the desk at the bank; one of old man Hoffmeister's nine boys leased the white farm-house built after the model of white houses in the Connecticut hills. Fred and Grace were off to fill a wooden shell on Chicago's fringe or to conciliate timidly earlier settlers in Roselle, New Jersey. Or, if Fred was obdurate, Grace resigned herself to the battle and then it must have been consoling to remember how simply the March sisters lived in "Little Women" and to hear how Miss Frances Willard deprecated the frivolities of the cities. William James could presently explain that "we are thus driven by the necessities of our condition to proclaim that condition admirable and to seek precedents for so proclaiming it," and ladies of New York or Boston, in the stinking constriction of railroad coaches, were likely to be told off-hand that society in Sioux City was just as refined as society in the East, and that the High School had been called just as good as Andover or Saint Paul's for Rob—but when it came to the question of Sue, it was probably better for her to go on East for a little finishing, and if Sue's father had risen to be President of the First National Bank, there might be a year in Europe. And meanwhile the Middle Western woman had quietly become a fixture on the American social chart, a shadowy Titaness, a terror to editors, the hope of missionary societies and the prey of lecturers. . . . Was she fabulous? No, but she existed rather as a symptom of America's increasing cheapness than as an attitude of womankind. Her performances were listlessly sanctioned by men whose covert emotionalism she openly and more courageously expressed in an instinctive envy of all that was free, cool or unhaltered in life, in art and affairs. She was an emblem, a grotesque shape in hot black silk, screaming threats at naked children in a clear river, with her companionable ministers and reformers at heel. The collapse of American thought excused her forays; all that had been finely stalwart in the Bostonian age had vanished, the reckless courage and self-willed individualism of Emerson, Thoreau and Channing, the deliberate cultivation of research into the motives, not the manners of human action. The confusion of morals with manners, apparently inherent in the world that speaks English, had helped the mental lassitude of the Americans to destroy what was honourable in the Bostonian tradition, and from the remains of that tradition welled a perfume of decay, cants and meaningless phrases: "the nobility of democracy," "social purity" and the like. In the weak hands of the Alcotts individualism ceased to be a sacred burden, save when it showed itself as a vague and vaguer aspiration toward some prettiness still severe in outline, the grim nymph who navigates above the swinging soldiery of the Shaw memorial tablet in Boston's self. This nymph hovered upon shoals of women shuffling and cawing in congresses of the World's Fair in 1893. Here the Titaness of the midlands was hostess to her more restrained sisters of the East and West. The ungainly women of little towns sidled among the gowns of receptions and shyly fingered bows and laces of opulent robes. A gorgeous materialism had made a cavern for voices of the nation and the noises blended in a roar.

THE TITANESS

Ambrose Bierce had already testified a good memory
of obscure French prose by noting in the *San Francisco
Examiner* that applause is the echo of a platitude. The
nation now hastened to applaud this prodigiousness of
white stucco pinned to iron between Chicago's smoky
breast and the blue water. Architects had paid a valiant compliment to the Beaux Arts, and mankind now
gaped at studded domes and classicized fronts in the best
mood of that school infesting Paris after the reign of
the vulgar, useful Baron Haussmann. French tourists
shrugged in the dining-room of the Hotel Richelieu.
All this had done service at their own exposition of 1889.
Could the Americans think of nothing fresher? Why
not vast wigwams? But there was a certain cleverness
in detail. The columns of the Fisheries Building
amused with their capitals of twining eels and lobsters.
There was dignity in the mass of the Agricultural Building with its Indian woman leaning on the challenging
bull before the entrance. By night Edison's perfected
bulbs dripped glitter on the shivering lagoons. Rockets
swam across faint stars. The Midway's shows and
bands roared wonderfully. Edwin Booth could not give
his promised season of Shakespeare, because he died in
June, but you could hear the metallic, just soprano of
Lillian Russell in *La Cigale* or shudder as the colonel's
daughter of "The Girl I Left behind Me" intoned the
Burial Service while Apaches whooped outside the stock-
ade and her father reserved a bullet to save his child
from rape—an effect which Henry George found most
distasteful, for the parent of the single tax could conceive art only as a vehicle for "good and noble" pur-

37

poses. But George was touched by the Fair. He stood one night with Charles Nolan, watching the crowds of the Midway, and dreamed aloud: the people had done all this! It was "of the people, by the people, for the people!" The lawyer argued: "No, most of the money was subscribed by rich men. The people had nothing to do with designing the buildings." The economist pulled his beard and sighed. Anyhow, the people were enjoying it, and his friend Altgeld would govern Illinois. Perhaps the Kingdom of God was a little nearer. He strolled among the crowds and scandalized a waiter at the Auditorium by demanding for late supper cold stewed tomatoes, sugared, while his host drank champagne. Materialism triumphed around him; Grover Cleveland had offered William Whitney a place in the Cabinet; nobody had protested the sending of troops to Buffalo, last year, to curb the strike in the railroad shops; Edward McGlynn had gone back to the Church of Rome and the reconciliation was announced quietly, after the awful tumults of the priest's excommunication in 1886. But there was hope in Altgeld and the People's Party, even if Cleveland had gone over to capitalism and McGlynn's social criticism would henceforth be limited to the admonitions of a formal creed. The Prophet drifted through the show, shook hands with Mrs. Potter Palmer at the Women's Building into which she had somewhere driven a nail of precious metals, and then he vanished eastward, courting no notice.

But clamour filled the ears of ticket-sellers on the morning of June 22nd. That day all California seemed rushing westward, bound for the funeral of Leland Stan-

ford, whom Henry George had denounced as an able
thief. The immense man lay dead in Palo Alto suddenly. He had never been unpopular in his State.
The easy casuistry which protected all the railroad-
builders had peculiarly worked on his behalf, and he had
been genial, truly kind. He tossed gold coin to news-
boys on the streets of Washington; his dinners were royal;
his stable thrilled sportsmen; he had given the State a
complete university in the memory of his only child, and
after that criticism swooned into a mere mutter. But no
kindness woke in the being of Mrs. Ida Channing
Walker, lately landed at San Francisco with her niece
after an inspection of Japan. She wrote a denunciation
of Stanford, not the financier, but the "winebibber,
atheist and horse-racer" and sent it by messenger to
the *Chronicle*, which failed to print it. Mrs. Walker
persevered and in person visited the offices of journals.
Editors were deaf. The man was unburied and flags
of San Francisco flew at half-mast for him. Her shamed
and frightened niece implored Mrs. Walker to be still
and then found an ally in a young Methodist preacher
when her aunt decided to attend the funeral and call
attention vocally to Stanford's defects. The preacher
wrought powerfully and in some way deflected Mrs.
Walker's zeal. She took a train for Chicago, and Leland Stanford was buried in peace. . . . He lies with
his wife and son in a temple of slick grey stone under the
patronage of a superb oak-tree. The tomb is guarded
before by two male sphinxes of Semitic aspect and at
the rear by two female sphinxes wearing Florentine
necklaces. The right-hand sphinx is obviously insane

and her eyes glare furiously at a barrier of foliage as if it hid some enemy. Beyond this silent corner of the park, lads with hair bleached by perpetual sunshine swirl in fast motors and profanely flaunt jerseys of cardinal red, as though death and judgment did not matter much.

Besides Mrs. Walker, battalions of the virtuous now appeared at the Fair. Congress after congress for the correction of mankind drew ladies to galleries. Walter Besant, an English writer, described literature as engaged in social tasks with a new sobriety and purpose. There were ripplings and shiverings while E. T. Gerry assured the Purity Congress that prostitution existed in the United States and that abominable practices among Romish choirboys had been rumoured. Susan Anthony and Frances Willard congratulated the new Anti-Saloon League. Celebrities gleamed in frocks with ruffled sleeves at receptions of the Woman's Club. Provincial gentlewomen might stare upon the gowns of Mrs. Potter Palmer or Mrs. Charles Henrotin and then shift their adoration to Mrs. Frances Hodgson Burnett, mother of "Little Lord Fauntleroy" and lately mother of "One I Knew the Best of All" in *Scribner's Magazine*, a graceful summary of her English childhood which fascinated William James and S. Weir Mitchell but found thin sales with her usual audience. So presently mothers trapped restless offspring and read to them the record of Mrs. Burnett's return to her stall in the sugar market with "Two Little Pilgrims," which tells how two quaint and fanciful children went to the beautiful World's Fair and were adopted by the kindest rich gentleman. Then there was the quiet, dry woman known as "Octave

Thanet" who soon would assert that American women in crowds lost their manners. And always there was Frances Willard, whose shrine was in Chicago.

Women celebrated in other capacities might be seen. Amused journalists of New Orleans chatted with their city's leading procuress, who had brought her entire stock, suitably costumed, on a holiday to broaden their minds. And there was the aureate creature of whom Mark Twain lazily remarked that the average man would rather behold her nakedness than Ulysses Grant in his full dress uniform. Indeed, ladies wearing white ribbons besought the Mayor of Chicago to exclude painted women from the Fair's grounds, but uselessly. So in that city, on the night of July 5th, as it slumbered under the doubled protection of Mrs. Palmer and Miss Willard, there came the birth of an American folksong. The agent of a New York bank was roused and brought hastily to room 202 in a packed hotel. The room held a priest, some doctors, a handsome, scared lad from a small town in Iowa who blubbered that the lady just told him she was taking some headache medicine, and the bared body of a wonderful woman stretched on a bed in the muscular torments that follow a dose of strong poison. There was also a purse that enclosed a startling bankbook and some cards. The adolescent knew nothing. She had spoken to him on the Midway at the Fair. They let him go. The priest prayed and the body stirred until dawn. Delicate and just audible, voices filled the room and there came the scents of Jockey Club and heliotrope, the fluttering whisper of laces, the chuckled gossip of "The Black Crook's" dressing-room.

. . . Kitty, did y'see Jim Fisk's sleigh with the silver bells yest'day? . . . Say, Kitty, who gave you the house in Twelfth Street? Honest, Kitty, I won't tell! . . . Kitty! Kitty, Ned Stokes shot Jimmy over at the Grand Central an' the p'lice are lookin' for Josie Mansfield! . . . These astral echoes floated over the fair body until it loathsomely stiffened on the bed. And then something slim and exquisite rose in a cloud from the sagging wreck. She stood preening the ruffles and the slanting hat in which Brady photographed her for the delight of bucks along Broadway in 1869. She hitched tighter to the famous ankles her striped Watteau stockings and her feet that once ran bare across bogs in County Clare now tripped in those ridiculous little shoes from which men drank champagne. Outside a misty door Kitty dawdled, a bit scared, uncertain in the gloom pierced by red shadows rolling up from Purgatory, and then a voice ineffably French murmured behind her: *"Ma toute belle!"* and Kitty turned to beam professionally on a delicious gentleman, smartly groomed once more, whose grin suggested release from some sharp agony. They looked and liked. The gallant blond fellow tucked under one arm a ghostly advance copy of M. Pierre Louys's *Songs of Bilitis*, not yet published, after turning down the page at . . . *"Mon dernier amant, ce sera toi, je le sais. Voici ma bouche, pour laquelle un peuple a pâli de désir. . . ."* and pretty Kitty went down the ordained steps with Guy de Maupassant chattering tenderly in her ear, and now the ribald sing:

42

THE TITANESS

"In room Two Hundred and Two,
The walls keep talking to you.
Shall I tell you what they said?" . . .

And in New York a balance of more than three hundred thousand dollars acquired by a dancing-girl who didn't dance was split among her Irish kin. She was not yet forty. In Constantine perhaps Pierre Louys was polishing off, "*Se peut il que tout soit fini! Je n' ai pas encore vécu cinq fois huit années . . . et déjà voici ce qu'il faut dire: On n'aimera plus . . .*"

The Fair went on. Mr. John Pierpont Morgan stalked through the palace of Fine Arts and brutally remarked of the French exhibits that they seemed to have been picked by a committee of chambermaids. Indeed, artists were disappointed with the French exhibits, and that disappointment speaks in William Walton's official volume on the Fair's art. Where were the Impressionists? These Monets, Seurats and Renoirs cried up in the magazines weren't to be seen. Mr. Brownell had been describing the new movements in *Scribner's*, but where were the symptoms of all this fever? Instead, here was the full Academic tone and scope—military pieces, the inevitable Madeleine Lemaire, the inescapable Debat-Ponsan, the "Wasp's Nest" of William Bouguereau, lent by Charles Yerkes, a financier who had rightfully succeeded Bouguereau's first American patron, the gambling procurer "Cash" Brown. Mrs. Grace Ralston Lewis escorted party after party of rural folk through the galleries and was disgusted because the Iowans and Kansans would stop to stare at Edwin

43

Weeks' "Last Voyage," a dead Hindu rowed toward the burning ghat, in the American section, when they should have hurried to gaze at the Whistlers and Lord Leighton's "Garden of the Hesperides." She could not interest them in her favourite English painter, Ellen Terry's first husband, who had sent over as a free gift to the United States one of his best pictures. It showed the tanned captain of an Eton crew clad in an apron of misty shadow leading a naked but pretty imbecile up a slope of rock toward nowhere. The picture had already been displayed in America without popularity or comment. It was called "Love and Life." Mrs. Lewis, on her own admission, was then a rather sentimental person, lately wed, and she thought well of "Love and Life," but her guests and visitors weren't enthralled. It wasn't the nudity of Love or Life that annoyed them. They simply didn't care for Art in the rendition of George Frederick Watts. She recalls small outcries before the "Temptation" of Claude Bourgonnier, a very buxom trollop lolling on the shoulder of an addled Saint Anthony, and before Rosset-Granger's "Jetsam," a dead lady wallowing in the backwash of a wave on some Bohemian seashore. But nobody protested "Love and Life."

All through the '80's had risen a discussion of "the nude"—that soft, then hard insinuating syllable that nearly rhymes with "lewd." The nude had been denounced by Anthony Comstock and, of course, had been mentioned in his amazing "Traps for the Young." Will Low and Kenyon Cox had written conjointly a defence of the nude in *Scribner's*, the sounding-box of art in the '90's. At the World's Fair the artists who essayed the nude announced by every concession of wind-blown drapery, floating vegetable matter and opportune posture that they considered a naked body most obscene. As usual the statues were more daring than the pictures and, as usual, nobody cared. Paul Bartlett's completely naked Ghost Dancer was admired and people merely chuckled over Rudolph Maison's enthusiastically naked Negro bouncing on a donkey. Comstock had declared that "nude paintings and statues are the decoration of infamous resorts, and the law-abiding American will never admit them to the sacred confines of his home," forgetting comfortably that the Greek Slave of Hiram Powers had been copied and distributed freely years before and that a statue of George Washington dressed in nothing but a blanket constantly faced the Capitol at Washington. Elbert Hubbard wagered that Comstock would appear at Chicago and make himself heard against the Fine Arts. Comstock lost the bet for the fantastic editor. But another force moved. Mild paragraphs dotted the journals . . . " "a powerful organization of ladies" had protested the sending of "Love and Life" to Grover Cleveland. The papers were not specific. The ladies were "members of a society to promote tem-perance," or "some members of a semi-religious society headed by Miss Frances Willard of Chicago." Incor-rect versions blew about. The Young Women's Chris-tian Association was blamed, and so were the suffragists. Excitement broke out in the small artistic quarter of New York. A group of young artists, headed by Wil-liam Sonntag, went from editor to editor, until James

Gordon Bennett of the *Herald* told them blandly that he had no intention of fighting women and they broke up in discouragement. A pure and enlightened womanhood had won without a struggle.

3

The World's Fair definitely set afire the suffragists. Without doubt and in spite of some ferocious squabbles, Mrs. Potter Palmer and the Board of Lady Managers had shown great competence. At receptions of the Woman's Club in Chicago there had been a parade of quietly effective professional women—Jane Addams, Florence Hunt, Jane Logan and the rest. Suffrage now woke with a roar. Bills to enfranchise women were offered in New York and in other eastern States. There were speeches and canvassings. The Reverend John Buckley implored male voters to respect female moral superiority by making sure that it wouldn't be soiled and degraded by putting a bit of paper in a ballot box. The Honourable George Hoar begged the men to let female moral superiority purify politics by voting. Rebecca Harding Davis remarked in Philadelphia that "silly, superficial arguments" were being used on both sides, and declined to take part. The usual pointless insults were exchanged in drawing-rooms, and the usual number of intelligent gentlewomen were lied to and rebuffed by politicians at Albany. New York showed the excitement at its highest. The campaign faltered along and its written record displays all the reasons why, twenty years later, Inez Milholland remarked: "They

raised enemies for themselves in the clubs and whisky dis-
tilleries with every breath," for the question of woman's
moral superiority constantly took shape as a direct threat
of what woman would do to all these barkeepers and rich
men's clubs and the like, and in the midst of the mild
little tumult a certain Rose Lipschowsky got up on a
soap-box in Union Square to say violently: "Why
don't all these ladies do something to help the Garment
Workers' Union instead of saying how good and refined
they are?" She was much applauded, got down from
her soap-box and vanishes altogether, an unconscious
symbol of what suffrage in the '90's omitted from its
speeches and programs. It would be a long time yet
before a woman would ask in print: "Are women people?" and it is in character that Alice Duer's career in
prose began with the fable of an undecided nymph and
a cynical owl. The suffragists of the '90's, if it's fair
to quote the words of their representatives, were on another tack. They were not people; they were "women,
trained by the essence of our natures to deeds of moral
elevation, education and the work of God!" This moral
superiority, Frances Willard wrote in 1892, had been a
thousand times declared by the mouth of man. And so
it had. But one sees curiously little about moral superiority in Constance Cary Harrison's novel, "A Bachelor
Maid," written in the winter of 1893 with her customary
smoothness. Mrs. Harrison's principal treasure was a
hatred of fools. She interrupted work one afternoon to
see some callers. One of them, a heavily moral young
matron, observed about a girl of good family lately
mother of an illegitimate baby: "She's behaved like a

woman of the working-class!" Mrs. Harrison mildly gazed at this idiot and mildly drawled: "I believe that illegitimate babies are arranged for in just the same way in all classes, my dear!" and signalled Mrs. William Tod Helmuth to remove this creature from her sight. "A Bachelor Maid" says neither Yes nor No to suffrage. It is competent light satire—the professional suffragist of the tale is an ignoble fraud sketched from a specimen that floated close to Mrs. Harrison's hand; there is suitable demonstration that woman's place isn't always the home. This is merely clever journalism and it had no chance of much discussion, for *Harper's Magazine* was publishing "Trilby."

With "Trilby" there came a sudden exposition of American woman. Du Maurier's drawings had always been published in *Harper's* and the house had brought out "Peter Ibbetson" in 1891. This second novel began with the January number of 1893 and instantly came storm, cancellations of subscriptions, and an increase of circulation. In June a jeweller produced a scarfpin, Trilby's foot in gold or silver, and women wore the badge. The soul of James McNeill Whistler was riven by Du Maurier's sketch of himself. He protested aloud and the cartoonist let the portrait be suppressed when the novel was published. The critics saw that this was Thackeray in solution, but a craze had begun among women and now comedians in light opera asked each other: "Where's Mamie? . . . Upstairs reading 'Trilby'?" and feet and shoes were suddenly "Trilbies" while ladies in the beginning literary clubs debated Trilby's ethics and clergymen regretted to point out to fashionable parishes that Mr. Du Maurier was no Christian. Harper's Brothers paid royalties on edition after edition. Virgins posed as Trilby in her Greek gown in the tableaux of two winters. A bathsuit, a cigarette, a cigar and a restaurant were named for Du Maurier's marshmallow goddess. Suffrage got tangled with the question of nude art. Trilby had something to do with woman's independence. Saint Gaudens said airily at a male dinner party: "Every other woman you meet thinks she could be an artist's model," and the hunchbacked Paul Leicester Ford wanted to know of the same group: "What would happen to an American if he'd written 'Trilby'?"

The question was unfair. But young John Ford Bemis was just then finding out what happens to an American novel in which conventional religion is mocked no more sharply than Du Maurier had mocked it in "Trilby." He had written on his uncle's farm in Georgia the story of a preacher named John Orme who took to reading history and then collapsed into agnosticism. He was driven from his church and sat enjoying Kant in a hut beside a swamp, after his wife had abandoned him in the name of Christ. She returned as a mob came to lynch him after the tumult of a camp-meeting near by. The pious chased the pair into the swamp and slaughtered them. Their bodies sank into the muck, the symbol of modern religion. All this was told nimbly and discreetly in the manner of Bret Harte. Mr. Bemis sent it to his mother's friend Frank R. Stockton for approval. Stockton advised: "You had best get the couple out of the swamp alive, but your conclusion is logical and right." He recommended the book to the *Century*. Richard Gilder wrote, when returning the manuscript, a kind, long letter explaining that the *Century's* large domestic circulation wouldn't receive this story placidly. *Lippincott's Magazine*, able to publish Oscar Wilde's "The Picture of Dorian Gray," was afraid of the "religious element" in the American book. For *Harper's Weekly*, Henry Mills Alden wrote: "Would it not be possible to mitigate the final scenes? Is it strictly necessary that Mrs. Orme should die with her husband? We have so many ladies on the list of our subscribers. . . ." Mr. Bemis came up to fight for his infant. Alden and Charles Dudley Warner were firmly kind. Yes, to be sure, "Trilby" contained agnosticism, an unhappy ending and some harlotry to boot, but— Well, Mr. Bemis had an income. His novel could wait. It is dismoded, now, but it had many merits for the day and he retired from letters with that sense of the sewer which will float among American writers for a long time yet, perhaps. He didn't recognize that Paris is the Amneran Heath of the American woman on which anything is likely to happen, and that the legend of a naked woman beside the Seine was safe from that certain censorship of the Titaness.

This question of American woman and letters seems to have been much debated just then and Charles Nolan fell foul of the shrewd Julian Ralph in an argument on a steamer. Ralph assured him that editors were really bothered and often insulted by notes from women and when the lawyer hooted the idea Ralph proved his point

by collecting twenty-five specimens of abuse addressed
to *Harper's*, the *Century* and, it seems, to *Lippincott's*.
Three letters are dated from New York. The rest came
from Ohio, Illinois, Indiana and Kentucky. The main
topics of objurgation are three. . . . A nice woman has
been killed or failed of marrying the right man in some
story. Liquor, including beer and claret, has been drunk
by otherwise respectable people or has been mentioned
without assault in an article. The story teaches nothing. In six of these letters the name of Louisa Alcott
is cited as a proper writer and to one of them is signed
the name of Frances Willard. By way of minor complaint one learns that John Fox's "A Cumberland Ven-
detta" has ungrammatical passages and contains coarse
language unsuited to growing boys, that Lester Raynor's
tale of the intriguing Mrs. Deepwater who arranged her
dinners by getting in one celebrity to meet another is an
insult to "Western womanhood," that it is "disgusting
and unmanly" to mention the Pope in an article contain-
ing the name of Edward McGlynn, author of "The Pope
in Politics," and that the words "breasts," "belly,"
"damn," "vomit," and "rape" are unfit for Christian
women to read. The one attack on "Trilby" is signed
by Ada Channing Walker, whose activities were now
ending. She had lately discovered that William Whitney was a horse-racer and had written Grover Cleveland
to oust him from the Democratic Party without getting
satisfaction. So she drew up a document on marriage
for her niece, advising her to marry only a man resembling "our precious Saviour, Jesus Christ, in manners and

appearance." Unable to do so, from lack of data, the girl mourned her aunt two months and married a sugar broker, six feet three inches long.

A trait binds these letters: they are dated directly on the offence. Emotion took up a pen and wrote on the best paper. There is not a trace of intellectual process. They were annoyed; etiquette had been battered or an opinion expressed that they didn't like. It is the voice of the porch shaded by dusty maples along Grand Avenue in a hundred towns, a resolute violence of the cheapest kind, without breeding, without taste. And there comes, too, a hint of the slow battle between the city and the small town. "You people in New York" are doing thus and so. "I suppose," said Mrs. Janette B. Frobisher, "the society women in New York like to read swear words, but——" . . . And yet in Bucyrus, Ohio, a copy of Zola's "Nana" went from soft hand to soft hand until it came back to its owner in the state of a worn Bible and slim fingers stained the pages of a tall "Salammbô" opposite to the plate of Matho squatting with his head against the knees of the Princess, who cried out: "Moloch, thou burnest me!" while the kisses of the warrior, Gustave Flaubert said, seared her body, more biting than flames. However, he was French. From France, too, came the monotone of a querulous oboe, languidly reciting how sure pain was, how fleet light love in Constantine or Nagasaki. He had joined Mrs. Humphry Ward in rejecting the sacraments, but then he mourned so prettily: "O Christ of those who weep, O calm white Virgin, O all adorable myths that nothing will replace, you who make tears to run more gently, you who show your smile at the edge of death's black trench, you alone give courage to live on to childless mothers and sons motherless, be ye blessed! And we who have for ever lost you kiss while weeping the prints left by your tread as it moves from us." So an untidy infant at play in a park owned and managed by a fat squirrel named James G. Blaine concluded that Mr. Loti was a great ladies' man, probably one of those who sometimes sang of their darling Clementine at night behind red nipples of cigars, beside a moonlit cottonwood, rustling over laughter and music of guitars. . . .

But if you were a proper editor, bred in the society of Newark or of Hartford, you did not trifle with the Titaness and for her sake you issued tales of women, by women, for women, in which one discovers the strangest things about that duel of the sexes, a deal discussed in the '90's. It would be fun to know what Sarah Jewett, Agnes Repplier or Margaret Deland thought of stories printed alongside their work. The voice of Louisa Alcott echoes in these tales: Alice Perrine on a trip to Boston found that her betrothed had once tried to kiss the pretty wife of a professor during a dance. He is given no chance to explain. Tears dribble on a box which takes his ring back to him: Miss Cornwall finds that her lover once wooed a girl who scorned him. The other girl is now very sorry. Miss Cornwall, allegedly fond of her swain, simply packs him off to his former fancy. The gentleman gulps and goes to his doom. Another Miss Cornwall finds her affianced once lived, ten years before, in Rome, with "a woman." He is dispatched to find and marry the girl, and "with

bowed head, he faced the long path of his duty."
Charles Milton's lungs have sent him to California,
orange-growing, and he is very comfortable and prosperous. But his wife yearns for Boston, the scene of her
girlhood, and on finding that out he simply sells the
orange grove and takes her home, "for he had learned
what he owed to her womanhood at last." And again
you hear Louisa Alcott in tales of Aunt Semanthy and
Cousin Hetty from the country who set the frivolous city
folk to rights with advice and chicken broth, flatteries
of the farm against the triumphant urban women whose
photographs spotted the *New York Herald*, whose balls
were detailed in a dozen journals of widest circulation.

Now too there appeared, sparsely, another fictional
flattery of women, often written by men, in which young
girls decide the winning of great football matches by
sending some player a violet at the right second, in which
maidens repel and crush a male animal in high lust by a
simple stare of wonder, in which the female principal is
risen above romance and becomes an opalescent cloud,
dripping odours which had nothing to do with the pro-
cesses of childbearing at all . . . and concurrently in
Chicago a living lawyer was consulted by a young woman
of fashion about a marriage contract in which her husband would pledge himself not to consummate the marriage. He reported this to a friend of his calling in New
York, and on March 9, 1898, found that the metropolitan lawyer had already been consulted about a dozen
such contracts. A few months before, in England,
George Bernard Shaw had inquired whether it was true

that American women really liked to be worshipped on false pretences.

Did they? It has been argued that an extraordinary deference to women began in America with the sexual starvation of the colonial time. In 1709 some cynic named E. Lea wrote, on the margin of a "Venice Preserved," that "I did see in New York for 8 years together that any punk may marry her well who had not her calling too rank on her face, so strong the men were to wive." And that phenomenon against prudery occurs in all colonized societies. Scarcity excuses the offered article. E. Lea's notation simply records the obvious source of innumerable American, Canadian and Australian families. But with the nineteenth century that situation had altered; in the East old maids were plentiful. As the century waned, all the European ills had arrived. Prostitution had increased immensely. Female workers in the industrial centres were abominably paid although associations mostly organized by foreign Jewesses had a little improved the condition in New York and Chicago. The farmer's wife continued to raise welts of muscle along her arms beside the sink and in the garden. In the South, ladies of place smiled as Sphinxes smile when told by Northern tourists that they lacked practical gifts, and went on planning gowns to last three years, writing sketches for newspapers and subtly urging their men out of the stagnation then changing its colours. Everywhere, the schoolteacher starved along on disgusting wages. But for the woman of any means a terrific machine of flatteries had been patented. Her social importance had climbed higher and higher since the Civil War and in the following twenty years of rank commerce. There was no longer any talk of hosts in the great cities: social columns announced the acts of hostesses. The men were too busy to bother. The men were too busy to bother with their own homes, and with the '90's they were suddenly informed of woman's power. A spattering foam of satire flecked new comic weeklies—*Puck*, *Life*, *Judge*, *Truth*. Women, it seemed, were bullying husbands and fathers for money to be spent on frocks, French tenors, flowers for actresses and actors. Women were listening to Oriental philosophers and reformers, sitting to expensive painters, running abroad to hunt down titled Europeans, gouging man's eyes out with hatpins, hiding his view of the stage at plays with vast hats, adorning his house with costly gewgaws, making him damned miserable in all ways.

In 1895 the neurologist S. Weir Mitchell wrote to a dead man of his dead wife: "You are entirely responsible for Mrs. . . . 's condition. I say so on your own admissions to the effect that you have accustomed her to spend money on herself and your daughters without stint and met all her demands in the way of entertainment. I am tired of writing letters such as this, for the tendency of American men to leave the management of their homes and families to their wives without advice or supervision is growing malignant in its results. Mrs. . . . now feels herself deeply aggrieved by your interference and her condition is dangerous in the extreme. A meaningless and injudicious deference to her wishes has done the harm. . . . I advise a permanent

separation." A meaningless deference to the wishes of
Mrs. . . . had caused her to tear down a superb
Georgian house while her husband was abroad and to
order the erection of a French manor in white stone which
hideously existed until it happened to burn ten years
after the psychiatrist's advice.

Indeed it was a singularity of the Titaness that she
had quite succumbed to all exterior ornaments of France
and every summer saw her in augmenting swarms as she
invaded the world's most successful shop, acquiring ster-
eotyped clothes, furniture, attentions and parasites with
that wide-eyed credulity which remains her great excuse
and charm. Richard Harding Davis saw her browbeat-
ing bandmasters for American tunes, just as he had seen
her romping and running races in staid English hotels,
and brotherly gave her warning that relatives of a French
husband would hold her beauty small and herself no
better than the Indian squaw whose voice she possessed,
whose dignity she has not yet assumed. But Mamma
and the Girls were abroad to see the world, and it was
theirs. Europe beheld them jamming past the guardians
of secret, obscene galleries in Naples, set there to guard
their famed innocence; they aimed cameras at William
Hohenzollern, Donatello's simpering David and the
Prince of Wales with equal zest. In spring they flooded
New York's marmoreal hotels, waving steamer tickets
from table to table and threatening to meet each other in
London, and autumn saw them home again, radiant in
fresh frocks, hats rejected by the prostitutes of Paris as
too gaudy for their use. So Charles Dana Gibson por-
trayed his Mr. Pipp, bullied all across Europe by Mother

and the Girls, these last a pair of goddesses, certain of admiration everywhere, miraculously sprung from ugliness. For the American Girl had been invented. The saponaceous *New York Herald* announced her as "better dressed, better mannered, more lovable and lovelier than any maiden of Europe," and now she glowed in coloured calendars, on the lids of candy boxes and the covers of magazines, more and more vividly as the decade wilted down. There came the Gibson Girl, the Christy Girl, the Gilbert Girl, and the paler, more subtle virgins of Henry Hutt, the slim patrician girls of Albert Wenzell—a parade of incredibly handsome, smartly dressed young things without existence anywhere. The beauty of two Englishwomen, Mary Mannering and Julia Marlowe, was set in rings of roses on pasteboard to show Flowers of the American Stage. The exquisite Julia Arthur, a Canadian of Irish parentage, was announced as "the supreme bloom of our national beauty" when she conquered the critics in "A Lady of Quality," which proved that the best way of ending an illicit love is to brain your paramour with a riding-crop. But Paul du Chaillu went hunting across New York for "those women that I see in your newspapers" and seems to have been slightly disappointed in the results of his chase. The commercial worth of these flatteries has been quite forgotten by critics, native and foreign, who have chattered of a feminized society. "In America," wrote Aline Gorren in 1899, "it is the business of the artist, the shopkeeper and the publisher to show vain women an improved photograph of themselves." And to the improvement of that photograph had been added the suppression of all other images. Adept lecturers promulgated the notion of a native literature pruned for the benefit of the virgin and the sedate matron, who were reading Alphonse Daudet's *Sapho*, D'Annunzio's "Triumph of Death," Rudyard Kipling's "Light That Failed" and "Love o' Women." It could be proved by Hamilton Wright Mabie that Tolstoy's "Resurrection" was admirable and worthy the attention of any lady, but that Stephen Crane's "George's Mother" was "harsh and unnecessarily frank" even after the phrase "for he had known women of the city's painted legions" had been stricken from its third chapter. The Titaness in the garments of Cybele must be placated as the priests of the Great Mother were wont to do. William Winter would lash the playwrights in her behalf and at the first night of "Arizona" Acton Davies would find himself surrounded by a band of ladies denouncing Augustus Thomas for his picture of the sullen, bored officer's wife, tired of the desert, ready to elope with a lover in whom she has no belief. Even Pierre Berton's "Zaza" would be tagged with a last scene showing the strumpet redeemed, successfully regnant as a great actress.

Then, and on March 1, 1900, a version of "Sappho" was produced at the Casino theatre in New York. Clyde Fitch had softened the tale carefully. Fanny Legrand was no longer a woman on the edge of age, hunting a lover, but a goddess, applauded as she came down a staircase, to music, by the guests of the masked ball. Miss Olga Nethersole, the English actress who appeared as Fanny, had already pained William Winter by kissing actors on the mouth in "Carmen," and now there rose a scandal when she permitted her leading man, an excellent amateur photographer, to lug her bodily up winding steps to a theoretic bedroom at the end of the first act. The curtain fell for a minute, and then Jean Gaussin was shown descending in the light of dawn to a twitter of zinc birds in the wings. Horrible noises ensued. Miss Nethersole was bullied by the press and arraigned in court for indecency. A committee of gentlewomen gathered at the house of Mrs. William Sonntag and hastily wrote a petition to the Mayor of New York stating that "the version of this novel is in no respect obscene and is in fact milder than the novel itself, which has had free circulation in the United States. Miss Nethersole's performance is entirely proper and restrained. . . . It is derogatory of the public intelligence that a celebrated work of art should be altered or expurgated. . . . Since this prosecution has been asked in the name of American women, we find it necessary to protest." The petition was circulated for two days and signed by suffragists, writers and women of the smart world. The prosecution had already become silly. Miss Nethersole was acquitted; the play went on. Ladies stormed the theatre. William Winter was horribly upset. But on April 4th a minor actor in the company received a note from the head mistress of a school for girls in the Hudson valley, requesting him to remove his daughter, a child of eleven, "as several mothers of several students have seen the play in which you are appearing and they cannot consider Margaret a fit companion for their daughters in consequence. . . ."

It is not alleged against the women of the Mauve Deccade that they invented cheap cruelty and low social pressures, but they erected these basenesses into virtues by some defensive sense of rectitude, and a generation of sons was reared in the shadow of the Titaness, aware of her power, protected by nothing from her shrill admonitions. Is it matter for such wonder among critics that only satire can describe this American of our time who drifts toward middle age without valour, charm or honour?

WASTED LAND

SIR RICHARD BURTON's last American visitor was an intrepid lady who once had been a reporter in New York when the calling was held unfit for women and their summaries of balls, religious meetings or such things were sent by messenger to profane offices of Park Row. Burton began by being rude to Mrs. Beach. American writers, he remarked, were a pack of muffs; the publishers —particularly his own—and the critics made up another pack. He stormed at his guest until it proved that she came from California. His sympathy was then as tedious as his rudeness. Why was nothing written about the West? In some room of his intellectual warehouse he had stored a mass of facts in Western history and scandal. Mrs. Beach finally fled from the surge of questions and before she reached London, homeward-bound, the adventurer was dead—on October 13, 1890, leaving his translation of "The Scented Garden" in the clean hands of Isabel, his wife, who promptly burned it without pausing to think that he had already ruined the fame of two celebrated obscene works by simply rendering them into English. Her silliness caused a deal of trouble, but French booksellers profited by selling *Le Jardin Parfumé* to Americans who never would have heard of it save for Lady Burton's prudery.

Mrs. Beach gave her report of Burton on American

affairs to the journals when she landed at New York
and failed to sell her unabridged article. Eastern
editors were then rather averse to printing rude observa-
tions on themselves, and Burton's comment came belated.
The West was suddenly a subject in 1891. The
Century brought out notes on primitive California and
a tale of Hamlin Garland. Julian Ralph's careful reports of Western States and cities appeared in *Harper's*.
Frederick Remington's sketches and the first of Owen
Wister's stories found attention. The wave of interest
lasted through 1892 with a froth of politics as the young
People's Party began to boil and essays on the farmers
of the midlands, on the railroads and rural banks were
printed in the *Arena*, a magazine that seems to have had
at least one devoted reader, Theodore Roosevelt. The
wave sped among obituaries. Eminent people were
dying in groups. Herman Melville, George Ernest
Marie Boulanger, Charles Stewart Parnell, Edward
Bulwer Lytton, author of "Lucile," James Russell
Lowell, Cardinal Manning, the Duke of Clarence and
Avondale, betrothed to a Princess of Teck who married
somebody else, Edward Freeman, Walt Whitman,
William Astor, Manoel Deodora da Fonseca, George
William Curtis, and John Greenleaf Whittier all had
vanished to appropriate music of the journals before
incredible persons such as those who weep in theatres
and build tombs invited clergymen to pray for the health
of Alfred, Lord Tennyson. Prayers were offered in
several American cities as September of 1892 ended.
All the worst of Tennyson's poems were known by
heart in the United States while Thomas Wentworth

Higginson vainly tried to have the tidal verses of "Ulysses" taught in the public schools of Boston, asserting almost piteously that a poet should be known by his best work and not by his weakest. Notes on the failing man's condition dotted the Eastern newspapers. The illiterate West, however, prepared an escort.

At half past nine on the bright morning of October 5, 1892, a lad named John Sibert was helping his aunt to wash dishes in a house of Coffeyville, Kansas. He had arrived in the little city two days before and was leaving Coffeyville on the train at noon. Coffeyville had two topics, that week; the main street was torn up for new drains and somebody had told somebody else from saddle to saddle on the prairie that Bob Dalton had bragged he would raid his own town in broad daylight. At half past nine, then, John Sibert was helping to wash dishes diligently. Between that moment and the second of twenty-five minutes to ten, rifles crashed. John leaped down his aunt's steps and slid against a post, smashing his watch. Some lad ran past him yelling: "The Daltons are in!" and the word reached a clerk at the station. In a few minutes men in Omaha and Kansas City were shouting the news as the one word, "Dalton, Dalton, Dalton, Dalton . . ." clicked from the keys all through the midlands. John Sibert loped around a corner and suddenly faced two long, grave young men with rifles in their hands. He didn't know Bob and Emmett Dalton from any other strangers and he started to ask something. Bob drawled: "Keep away from here, bud, or you'll get hurt," and shoved the boy aside placidly, then placidly strolled along with Emmett, snapping his fingers and whistling through his teeth. At once a lad named Luke Baldwin hurried into sight and didn't pause when one of the brothers shouted to him. Bob Dalton killed him forthwith and the pair trotted from John Sibert's view. . . . The famous gang rode into town at half past nine. They left their horses in an alley and calmly strolled up to separate in the space before the town's two banks. Bob and Emmett plundered one bank. Grattan Dalton with the henchmen Bill Powers and Dick Broadwell * attended to the other. Citizens grabbed the rifles with which the antecinemic West did its serious shooting and the fight began. Bright spires of glass toppled from frames of windows; smoke went in surges along the street as men fired busily from porches or through doorways. There are a hundred legends of what happened. Young John Sibert knelt beside the dying boy in the alley behind one bank and heard a man named Gump swearing in the pain of a shattered hand. Presently Broadwell rode wildly down the street with his hands gripped on the horn of his great Mexican saddle and fell dead from his mount a little way from the noisy town. Somebody killed Bill Powers. Grattan Dalton ran down the sidewalk with blood on his face and paused to rip the green handkerchief from his throat in full range of the batteries before he turned at the corner of a stable and fired back, killing the city's marshal with a superb shot from the hip. His shoulder was riddled so that he couldn't lift his rifle. He lurched from sight down the alley toward the tethered

* Called sometimes "Jack of Diamonds" from the song which he sang constantly. The song now passes as a "Negro melody."

horses. Bob Dalton strolled into view, loading his rifle, and a hundred muzzles were aimed at his blue shirt. One ball caught him above the navel but he walked on and sat on a heap of stones beside a barn, firing again. A man namel Kloehr ran from cover straight at the terrible rifle and shot the gang's captain in the lungs, then whirled and sent a bullet through Grattan Dalton's throat as the youngest brother crawled toward the plunging horses. Firing stopped. Men hurried up and a thick group formed around Bob Dalton in his carmine puddle on the clay. The body heaved in its blood but he kept yelling: "Ride!" Then someone howled and the crowd saw Emmett Dalton struggling among the horses. He was wounded four times when he got into his saddle and sat huddled with his gloves clasped on his groin. Men lowered their rifles, expecting him to fall, as men shot in the groin do, generally. But all the brothers were valiant. He spurred his horse down the alley and swung from the stirrups to seize Bob's arm. Politeness ended. Carey Seaman blew in his side with a fast shot. The last Dalton slid across his brother's body. It was now ten minutes to ten. Sightseers poured from trains before noon and the corpses of Lord Tennyson's escort to Walhalla were photographed so that it could be proved the Dalton gang was out of business after five years of graceful, even endearing performance. Unlike the James and Younger gangs, they didn't blow unarmed children to rags nor did they kill their mistresses in farewell as did the unlovable Tumlinson, once something of a hero. They were amiable and rather mannerly bandits, on the whole, and yet no ballad

69

bears on their name. The great tradition of Sturdevant, Murrel of "the mystic clan" in Andrew Jackson's reign, Boone Helm, Billy the Kid and Jesse James ended here in an alley on the crackling sound of Carey Seaman's shotgun. Jay Gould died eight weeks later in civilized New York, and in his bed.

The brothers had little notice in the East. Editors gave them a paragraph surrounded by notes on Grover Cleveland's latest speech or President Harrison's hopes. The West's main exhibit in October of 1892 was the dangerous People's Party. It demanded the governmental ownership of railroads and telegraphs, urged governmental banks for the use of farmers and upheld the issue of silver currency on terms making it almost the equal of gold. Not one of these notions happened to be strictly new but speakers of the young party assailed the railroads, their builders and owners, and the party swiftly became a cyclone whirling from Kansas or a scowling farmer in a cowboy's wide hat stretching predatory hands toward Washington. The dignified little essays of Hamlin Garland and the rest in the *Arena* were probably not read; the Populists naturally were "crazy" when mentioned in the journals. Edwin Godkin viewed them without sympathy. One editor who might have broadly taken their side was Joseph Pulitzer, whose wrath against Collis Huntington and other lords of the railways had been repeatedly in print. But only a few newspapers in New England condescended to treat the People's Party as a positive effort in social criticism and when four senators and eleven congressmen were elected from States in which Democrats and Populists had fused, there was a waver of real panic among the rich, those sons of the Golden Ass hopeless of rose-leaves to make them men. Some alarmed gentlemen interrupted Mark Hanna on a busy afternoon at Cleveland and asked him if they'd better sell their holdings in railroads at once. Hanna said amiably: "You make me think of a lot of scared hens." In New York a great lady proposed to John Kendrick Bangs that all the Populists be tried for treason. The humorist asked what the Westerners had done and the matron magnificently answered: "Everything!"

The Democratic triumph returned to his chair in Congress a tall, harshly beautiful young man from Nebraska named William Jennings Bryan and in Illinois a pallid, unconsciously emotional North German lawyer, John Altgeld, was elected governor. His success troubled the considerable Tory element, for it was known that he had the oddest notions of prisons, courts and popular rights. Senator John Macauley Palmer of Illinois had also irritated some Eastern editors by a speech of July 7th. The old soldier drawled for thirty minutes, damning the use of armed detectives—he chose to call them bravos and ruffians—by Andrew Carnegie's steel plant at Homestead in Pennsylvania. Ten lives had been lost at Homestead in the ugly battle between strikers and detectives. General Palmer went the length of protesting "these private armies" and of insisting that Carnegie's workmen had the right of considering themselves permanently employed and of demanding reasonable pay for their drudgery. . . . Conservatives looked westward with annoyance. Mr. Bryan was still unknown in the

East but Altgeld now replaced the People's Party as the demoniac shape essential to American journalism.

In New York Ward McAllister's star reached its zenith. He censored the lists of a famous ball and his importance was trumpeted everywhere across the country. The career that began with careful courtships of wealthy hosts now concluded in the domination of great hostesses. The dandy was solemnly reported in the *New York Herald*, the valet's guide to celebrity, as writing his memoirs. The Four Hundred, the balls of some man named Bradley Martin, Pink Teas and the attempt of youngsters to wear silken knee breeches at dances—all these matters were copied from paper to paper and delighted lumberjacks in Oregon. The timid ostentations of a possible three thousand men and women living in cramped, airless houses between two polluted rivers were advertised as though an aristocracy moved proudly through some customary ritual. Had it been equally advertised that these people admired paintings by Alexandre Cabanel, who might have learned his trade over again from Thomas Dewing, Edward Simmons or Kenyon Cox and stuck up views of clean French peasants flirting with a white horse, by Debat-Ponsan, nobody would have understood. Perhaps if the cynical dealer in wines who openly bragged of selling Algerian brews in French bottles to the best clubs had written his thoughts to the press, provincial editors might not have taken the Four Hundred so seriously. But the Four Hundred had been created, now, and New York was an extravagant shimmer that persisted in the general imagination as a drunken planet while a disastrous, earthly pageant moved in the middle West with John Altgeld for its standard-bearer. An antithesis of the coarsest kind had been arranged, by journalism, and Altgeld appeared as a bearded prophet pointing up wrathfully at a frieze of cruel, jewelled figures on a marble ledge, creatures not mundane or merely silly but a set of brutal gods. It could hardly be known in Nebraska that a gentle minority in this society would not meet the plunderers, the railroad kings and the low politicians whose affairs were parables from 1892 to 1896. The West saw a solid rank of the plutocracy—Collis Huntington and Matthew Quay arm in arm with women for whom the tribal name of "Mrs. Astorbilt" was invented in 1893. What the East thought of the West is less and less important to know or to record. But journalism changed the pale governor of Illinois into a Maritsakro, a divinity of snakes risen from hell, through Chicago, who pardoned anarchists duller than Ward McAllister out of prison, forbade Grover Cleveland to send troops into his State and his demoniac quality lasted until his person was replaced by another, taller man.

Grover Cleveland entered the White House. President Harrison departed. The World's Fair began in thunders of music and flurries of rockets. Immediate trouble overtook the procession. A triumphant Democratic party was split by instant quarrels. The government of British India suspended the free coinage of silver. American railroads stopped ordering new coaches for the traffic to the Fair from Mr. George Pullman's great company on the edge of Chicago. This gentleman was an amiable person enough who shaved his upper lip and wore a tuft of grizzled whisker on his slightly jutting chin. One day of May, 1893, he was showing some friends through his plant and happened to drop a paper. A wiry boy stepped from the unfinished bulk of a car and handed the paper back to his owner. Mr. Pullman smiled. The boy grinned. The grandee and a human item of his property met so and never saw each other again. The human item survives as a chemist of repute. His name can be Jim for this page. He was sixteen and his guardian uncle had let him come to Chicago from a tame farm in central Indiana. He boarded in Pullman, the model suburb approved by Frances Willard, as liquor was sold only to guests at the hotel, and the harlot had no booth. Young labourers went into the hideous city for diversion and returned to pure Pullman according to circumstance and temperament. Jim vanished from Pullman in June when the least valuable workmen were civilly discharged. News of a "financial depression" vaguely reached the human item, taking a holiday on his uncle's farm, telling envious young cousins in the barnyard how Buffalo Bill's elaborate hair flapped under his sombrero at the Coliseum and what Lillian Russell really looked like. Financial depression meant nothing much. Jim went back to Chicago and found that plants were hiring nobody. He was idle for five weeks and then, one of thousands, tramped off into the fields where hands would be wanted for the harvest. But the tanned men were not hiring many helpers.

In November, the item had learned that financial depression meant no drawers inside his frayed trousers and

a constant, increasing wonder as to what the Congress
was doing in Washington. The triumphant democracy
fought over tariffs and tinkered with currency. Jim
heard and read about silver standards and gold standards, issues of fresh bonds to meet the shortage of gold in
the Treasury. The panic was real, now. Notices of
failures and suicides, starvation among miners in Ohio
and the work for their relief by William McKinley,
prophecies of A. P. Gorman and Russell Sage were
printed side by side. Jim beamed at brakemen on freight
trains and intrigued for passage into Indiana. He re-
verted to agriculture in December.

In the harassed, lugubrious January of 1894, a solid,
quiet financier at Cleveland in Ohio spent some afternoons strolling with an old friend along mean streets and
letting bills pass quickly from his plump fingers into the
hands of shabby men lined at corners who nudged each
other, muttering: "Here's Mr. Hanna." No identity
had yet been yet manufactured for the placid person by
Alfred Henry Lewis and Homer Davenport. On January 28th he wrote to an attorney in New York: "The
situation here is terrible. We are not in as bad shape as
Chicago. H—— tells me that our friend B—— is in
a bad way and likely to go into bankruptcy. Take enclosed to him and tell him to hang on." The unhappy
B—— broke into tears at the sight of Mr. Hanna's abominable script on a cheque, and hung on.

The Senate and Congress wrangled over tariffs. David Hill damned the proposed income tax as unconstitu-
tional. Populists accused conservatives of taking bribes
to prevent the destruction of the McKinley tariff, and

the journals announced a strange affair called the Army of the Commonweal, headed by General Coxey. Coxey and his lieutenant, Kelly, were bringing a mob of unemployed workmen eastward to make Grover Cleveland do something for them. Fights between Commonwealers and sheriffs happened in Oregon and California. Men discharged from halted work on railroads in Oregon joined the army. In Chicago scores and hundreds of workmen discharged by the Pullman Palace Car Company were joining the American Railroad Union. The Union consented to arbitrate its fight with the Great Northern railroad and won most of its wishes. The newspapers congratulated both parties and went on announcing the approach of Coxey's Army. Workmen in Chicago were anticipating the fictions of O. Henry and Anatole France, just then, by insulting policemen or smashing windows so as to be jailed, fed and warmed. . . . In March the item Jim set off for the tannery of a cousin in Nebraska. He already liked to potter with acids and materials. But when he reached the tannery it was shut and his cousin was desperately trying to raise loans to tide himself through the depression. Other small employers and great farmers in Nebraska were miserably conferring with the Bank. Jim faced about with six dollars in his pocket and began a free navigation eastward. The fringe of Kelly's division of Coxey's army picked him up at Omaha where Eugene Debs came to shake hands with Kelly, in a white necktie. The army, now a comic feature of memoirs, travelled on toward Saint Louis amid the sorrows of hens and the alarm of housewives. Jim swung his legs from the rear of a car and listened to a mixture of misery and bravado. But the curious humour of American workmen still operated among these unwashed. They were literate and mostly young. What could Grover Cleveland do for them? Or Congress? They deserted Kelly in swarms at Saint Louis. Jim made northward with a Dutch lad in a hospitable caboose and his companion presented him to a Dutch family in an unchronicled region outside Chicago where stolid folk named Annekje and Dirk grew vegetables.

Mr. Pullman and his workmen were now in full quarrel. Pullman had "nothing to arbitrate." The nation roused to a situation in Chicago, where twenty-four railroads centred and vast yards exchanged a thousand kinds of freight. Mr. Pullman was handsomely begged to submit his case to arbitration or simply to restore the wages of last year to his shrunken forces. It has since been explained that the manufacturer's close friends were against an arbitration. The American Railroad Union, the mayors of cities adjacent, Civic Federations and simple millionaires urged Pullman to come to terms. Far away Ambrose Bierce paused in his rattle of wit against the Southern Pacific Railroad of California to remark that Mr. Pullman was a gentleman in the American definition only. "A gentleman," Bierce mentioned, "is a man who bathes and has never been in jail." He then resumed the heaving of liquid fire at the Southern Pacific, called the Octopus in the State whose capitol was its office. The Octopus had absorbed the Central Pacific and had decided that its debts in the sum of sixty million dollars ought to be slowly refunded, say at two per cent yearly for half a century. A bill to permit this emollient arrangement in favour of the Octopus was accordingly presented to Congress. . . . But outside Chicago the item Jim was tending vegetables in an embarrassment of adolescent pride. His Dutch hosts couldn't afford him. Nobody wanted to hire him in Chicago, where grown men were doing a day's work for a bowl of soup and a loud roaring in saloons followed each day's notice that Mr. Pullman wouldn't arbitrate. Then the whiskered paternalist discharged three members of a committee that pled with him while he fingered a black rubber ruler on his desk. Most of the workmen left struck in a body and the plant closed. Mark Hanna hammered a cigar to death in a club at Cleveland and said angrily: "What in God's name does Pullman think he's doing?" William McKinley sent his brother Abner and three lawyers of power to call on Pullman, who told them that the matter now rested with other powers than his. Abner McKinley, kind as his brother, turned and walked out of the manufacturer's house in a rage.

The parade of Coxey's army had ended in a pathetic scene at Washington, where Coxey and some of his attendants were arrested for walking on grass with intent to commit a demonstration below the bulbous dignity of the Capitol. But there was an uneasy stir in the warming air all around Chicago. A convention of the Railroad Union gave Pullman its opinion. Editors everywhere openly favoured the strikers. Pullman's aides were voluble in the newspapers. A week of June passed in suspense. Then the Union declared a sympathetic strike and Eugene Debs begged everybody to refrain from violence. The railroads were palsied on July 1st.

It was promptly said that managers of lines hired men to rip up tracks, burn freight and destroy switches so as to make the strikers unpopular. Marshals were sworn in. Men who would not strike were hammered on the head by somebody. Orators yelled in saloons. Useless injunctions forbade strikers to preach the strike to non-striking. James Sovereign, grand master of the Knights of Labour, pondered on ordering his immense forces to strike also. Altgeld now reared and commanded Grover Cleveland to keep the Federal troops out of Chicago. Cleveland retorted that the mails must be guarded and the troops came on. Real violence exploded twice in two weeks. Men charged the guard at the Monon depot and were killed. Cars smouldered in the huge yard of the Chicago, Burlington and Quincy Railroad. The strike spread westward into seven States and Californians grinned at the attorneys and counsellors of the Octopus emerging from long conferences in its office.

Federal troops and militia camped on the margin of the lake at Chicago expecting anything. Agents of the railroads passed quietly through crowds in the hungry city offering five dollars a day for workmen at yards and stations. One of these picked up the item Jim, who was getting tired of this "battle between the producing classes and the money power of the country" in a phrase of Eugene Debs, and had tramped into Chicago hopeful of a train moving eastward to Indiana. Could he get a place as brakeman on such a train? The agent gave him a card with the name of some foreman on it and sent him off to report at an office in the yards. Scudding down an alley, the boy ran into a group of men, one of them wearing an engineer's cap. In the dusk the boy mistook that cap for a token of employment and called out asking where he could find this foreman. The word "Scab!" rose. The group converged and then left the atomic Jim blind and comfortably senseless in the gutter. Next morning a soldier found him crawling but unaware of motion, a bloody wretchedness that moved by habit. . . . On July 17th they began to arrest Eugene Debs for violating untenable injunctions. He submitted with his customary good nature. The strike collapsed. The sympathy that had followed it was rather dashed by the plundering of freight and ruin of property effected by men who may have been strikers. But there was a sharp protest, even in Tory newspapers, when Mr. Debs was sentenced in December to six months in prison. The phrase "government by injunction" had been invented. The *Springfield Republican*, the *New York Evening Post*, the *Evening Transcript* of Boston and a dozen other conservative journals struck at the sentence as a dangerous precedent. Mr. Debs went to jail but the Supreme Court at least admitted the right of workmen to strike peacefully. The strike at Chicago began to collapse in latter July and presently Mr. Pullman opened his plant. Wages and prices rose once more. The panic waned and vanished. But the middle West had been scared in its vitals. Its industries had been battered; the farmer had suffered, unequally according to location, and little towns had seen suicides of their bankers and merchants. There was no social parade to cure memory of a sharp impression, and Republican speakers were busily telling men that unsettled conditions, low tariffs, experi-

ments in currency came of bad government. Other
speakers were pointing out that a government pliant to
the summons of railroads needed a bath. Altgeld was a
hero in a stormy cloud to thousands who had never seen
him. The commonplace journals professed to admire
Cleveland's intervention, as they admired his candid
threat to England in the next summer when he took up
the Venezuelan quarrel and alarmed Edwin Godkin so
that the editor wrote two essays against war, repeating
everything that Thackeray had said on the subject without improving the satirist's simple statement of soldiers
and murderers as interchangeable terms. These grand
concerns soared over the item Jim on his uncle's farm
while he read texts of chemistry. He still brushed his
hair low on the right temple to cover three inches of blue
scar, and lads swimming with him in a lazy creek admired
a healed gash across his shoulders that seems to have been
made by a knife. But his broken ankle mended and one
night of May, 1895, he was tramping comfortably alongside the tracks, a mile from his uncle's farm, when a train
slowed to a water tank and he saw "Pullman" in gilded
paint high on a car's side. Simultaneously he stumbled
on a provident half-brick. The contact of the brick with
the name on the moonlit car naturally followed. Damage to property of a great corporation is thus reported
long after date.

The Octopus came to glory in January of 1895. Its
bill in Congress was defeated and now the Californians
declared war on the amiable fish itself. Nobody denied
that the Southern Pacific had advertised California terrifically in the East. The *Overland Monthly* hinted that

politicians revolting against the Octopus did so in the hope of swift bribery. But Ambrose Bierce had gone to New York to carry on the battle from that vantage. Shares and bonds of a new railroad were sold and men of wealth gathered around the venture to protect it. Eastern magazines heartily applauded. The long war of the Californians seemed a success. The Octopus had cynically raised and lowered rates to suit the weather and the profit of crops. Ranchmen sent stuff to market behind mules rather than meet the startling expense of shipping fruit on the Southern Pacific. Joseph Pulitzer renewed his attacks on Collis Huntington in the *World*, dictating editorials from which his stenographers removed the oaths. A pleasant confusion existed in the Eastern mind between owners and promoters of the Western railroads and the military engineers, surveyors and draughtsmen who dragged and bullied the lines into being. The distinction between a Grenville Dodge, sweating in the deserts, and a Collis Huntington, contemplating the results in an office, was finally clear for a moment, and is now again forgotten.

The Octopus floated on conversations for some months. Dr. Barrett Wendell amused a party at dinner in Cambridge by comparing Collis Huntington to Bronson Alcott. The professor had a curious, arranged voice that may have covered an intense shyness. He observed that the railroad king and the philosopher were both Yankees from Connecticut, sons of small farmers. Both had been pedlars in their boyhood. Suppose that Alcott had taken his pack into the hidden West and discovered an ideal of service to humanity to be expressed by shipping it and its goods for small sums of cash, instead of lecturing to it on meaningless subjects? In 1900 the professor shocked reverent people by his criticisms of Alcott and appalled a lady who met him shortly after Huntington's funeral where the heavy scents of flowers had stifled her. "But the smell of sulphur wasn't noticeable?" Wendell inquired. It was accounted a heartless remark.

The assault on the railroads had continued, with rallies and silences, from 1892 through 1895. Many Populist speakers found themselves justified in their acts. Some lines figure little in the piled clippings of the campaign. James Hill was assailed less sharply than were the owners of the Southern Pacific. Nothing much was alleged against the great system now the Atchison, Topeka and Santa Fé Railroad although it had critics here and there. Some of this matter is unjust, of course, but the whole printed collection of logical attacks and useless tirades might excuse a cynical comment, more invasive of American sentiment than Barrett Wendell's gibe. What was offered in the '90's was the spectacle of the plain people attacking themselves, for the railroad builders were sons of the plain people, nursed in the manners of small towns and of farms. But it will not do to suggest that early studies in sophisticated milk or the pressure of a thumb on scales in a rural store had anything to do with the root of these accusations, true or false. For in 1896 an excellent voice recited that "the plain people, bred without guile at the knees of Christian women, alone can cleanse this land of tyranny."

Mark Hanna now impressed himself strongly on a number of Eastern politicians who came to Saint Louis in hot June. They seldom knew how to spell his name and often added a final "h." The man of affairs was not particularly visible. He cared nothing for oratory and himself was never eloquent. His position was simple. He proposed to get his friend McKinley nominated and to have him elected. McKinley would keep the tariff high where it was needed and wouldn't experiment with the international laws of banking. The little, religious candidate's political ideas were few. He had spoken manfully for reforms in civil service, for boards to arbitrate strikes, and he was honestly shocked by the manners of the Octopus. Having secured his nomination, Hanna retired quickly from sight in a mist of flying aides-de-camp. He expected the Democrats to nominate Richard Bland, a wordy friend of Free Silver who apparently believed in the supremacy of the United States to an amazing degree, for he is quoted as saying: "If America issues a currency that raises silver to be the equal of gold, the rest of the world will quickly follow our lead." Bland's mind had embraced Free Silver with the lust of a grammarian for a debatable verb. It was known that Altgeld had approved him in a general fashion. Hanna expected him to be nominated on July 1st but he sent some volunteer spies to report the tone of the crowd in the Coliseum at Chicago. The Republican impresario was surrounded by young midlanders, sons of his friends and sons of McKinley's friends. The Major was dear to them, and the core of the plutocracy's body-guard consisted of young lawyers, insurance agents, postmasters and mere "business men," few of whom had any near hope of being able to give their wives a second servant. Four of this body-guard dropped their affairs and went to Chicago. They provided themselves with tickets and sat awaiting the nomination of "Silver Dick" Bland. The Republican Convention had been, externally, tame enough. This hot, moist assembly at once developed symptoms of poisoning by strychnine, and the spies discovered that they were minions of a superior Octopus, or of an armed ogre. . . . An emotion had been subtly born in this wasted land beyond the notice of the Eastern journals which now judged it so jauntily. Muscles had ached too long beside restless kine and winters had rimmed in men to talk, talk endlessly of the banks, the railroads and the glittering rich. Free Silver? It was just a phrase. Their wives had fed the strays of Coxey's army. Middlemen had taken too much of their profits. Their sons had come home penniless and frayed from closed factories and offices. This emotion only wanted, now, a tragic hero. Mark Hanna had drawled, at Saint Louis, that any handsome man with a taste for making speeches ought to try politics. David Hill, who was ugly, made speeches immensely and the convention yelled with or against him when he sneered at Free Silver. Eastern Democrats were hissed by Populists in the galleries. The extraordinary A. P. Gorman was mentioned as a low bastard by a delegate from Iowa. Altgeld was not well and his pallor startled one Republican watcher passing close to him as the crowd poured out from a session of words and excitements. The convention tossed and sweltered. Richard Bland's fortune rocked along in the welter. Then a tall, trim delegate walked through a shout to the platform and his voice

stilled the crowd for forty minutes. Men rose everywhere. Mr. Bryan, a very handsome man who liked to
make speeches, had the floor. Mark Hanna's spies ripped
their path out through the herd gone mad in adoration
of this incarnate drum.

Mark Hanna was not the phlegmatic joss of caricatures. When he was told that ladies of small
Nebraskan towns admired Mr. Bryan, he threw a cigar
into a fire-place, briefly swore, and then resumed business. His position was less and less pleasant as the
National Silver Party and the People's Party swung behind Mr. Bryan with rejoicings, and not with much cash.
But in early August, asking no future favours, great
Democratic personages at New York handed cheques of
size to Hanna's inconspicuous messengers and one of them
said quite wildly: "Tell Mr. Hanna I'll turn Protestant
if he wants, so long as he licks this feller!" And then
on the first cool air of September came news of an Independent Democratic Party in assembly at Indianapolis.
These Gold Democrats nominated John Macauley Palmer, the critic of Andrew Carnegie, and men of the labour
unions sent their good wishes to the old soldier. Eastern
politicians were alarmed. Hanna was delighted. "The
general," he said, "will get about a hundred thousand
votes from Mr. Bryan." The general outdid the estimate.

It was now quite necessary to elect McKinley. The
Major's little court at Canton, Ohio, pored over Democratic speeches. A tall young lawyer, Julius Whiting,
wrote on September 3rd to a friend: "The best thing
would be to convince the voters that this Silver humbug

will bring on another panic." The impresario had already ordered that note in some pamphlets. He nodded when the letter from Canton was brought to him and said: "Make a placard out of that." So handbills headed "Free Silver Will Bring Another Panic" were liberally printed and went whirling along in boxes through the middle West. Printing had never been used to such effect or in such bulk as Hanna now used it. His lieutenant at Chicago, William Hahn, scoured the region for speakers. Volunteers from New York, even with notes of recommendation signed by Theodore Roosevelt and Cornelius Bliss, were declined in favour of drawling men who knew how to talk to farmers. Hanna sat as a comfortable shadow in the Major's car when the candidate went forth to speak, and gossiped with Herman Kohlsaat, who was present in a small, astonished group that heard McKinley decline to come to terms with the disreputable Matthew Quay. Hanna did not scold his candidate. Next day speakers were telling audiences in Illinois and Minnesota that Mr. McKinley had refused to promise Quay anything.

But the terrible drum of the Silver Knight sounded from city to city, and his beauty towered in the flare of torches while bands played *El Capitan*. Hanna had raised a drapery behind the Major of golden cornucopias and golden coins, harbingers of prosperity under a high tariff. Yet an emotion might be evoked against an emotion. So a train appeared, passing over shorn fields. Messengers hurried a day ahead of its coming. Men of the Grand Army brushed black hats and gilded badges, then marched down to await this train with its last platform smeared in flags. They stared up at generals, veterans of their war. Howard, the Christian soldier, gravely reminded them that the Major had hot coffee served to his men in trenches and camps. There was Sickles with his glorious moustache. Alger and Stewart leaned down to shake hands and blushing grandsons were pointed out to them. Bugles and cornets yelled old songs and set heels tramping so that dust shot up and eyes watered. What had been believed was true again, in the noise of bugles; Union was strength and to hell with the Democrats, at the sound of cornets. Ghosts rose and charged through the cold air, at this noise of voices and brass, and cheers followed the train away. But one dusk at a junction of Illinois, the young manager found the crowd cool to General Sickles and puzzled until a lad beckoned him around the station to another lighted train. Hanna took his cigar from his mouth and said blandly: "Don't you know that this is a blue Presbyterian district, son? All these women remember Sickles shot his wife's beau. Give 'em Howard." He smiled and climbed back into his own train. The crowd applauded General Howard. . . . After a while torn posters blew in the streets and the emotions sank away. Henry George cried: "Oh, what did it matter about Free Silver? It's too bad, too bad!" and went pacing up and down his rooms at Fort Hamilton in distress; the people had lost again! In the high, yellow dining-room of the Union League Club above Fifth Avenue, Theodore Roosevelt assured some men that Hanna had done remarkably well for an inexperienced person. One of his hearers choked and upset a glass.

Architecture in America was still nothing but a malady. The tradition of fine building was ruptured and sterile before the Civil War. A mania for the grandiose began in the '70's and continued more and more fruitfully in the '90's. Congress gave itself a library such as nobody had ever seen. A pillbox of white marble with a conical cap was ordered to contain the mortal part of Ulysses Grant, and James Huneker met the general's spectre tramping up and down before his last home, chewing a cigar and swearing. Monsters of shingle crawled on suburban lawns. Even the reviving Georgian lines were frothed over with illegitimate detail. The wondrous rich now employed the power of fairy hands to raise Florentine fronts ending in manorial windows that excluded air in summer, light in winter. The Westerners could bring little that was worthy from the learned East and it is miraculous that the worst models were left on the Atlantic coast. But Easterners quite rightly complained, and may still do so in all honesty, of the ugly Western cities. The West rather pathetically called attention to handsome marble banks and dignified public structures, behind masks of electric cable and pole. Its imperial aspirations bade America do a deal of building; hotels resembling ennobled bath-rooms without visible conveniences rose everywhere; in her "Van Cleve" Mary Watts has beautifully reported the banks approved by sons of German immigrants in the midland, and in "The Conquest of Canaan" Booth Tarkington comments on the rural German brewer's villa. These things were no worse than preposterous "suites" in New York, where, says Harry Leon Wilson, sedate French violinists were mellowed into playing ragtime at dinners of the barbarous Westerners then invading Manhattan.

It is only in "The Spenders" that a vision of the movement from West to East survives out of the '90's. For there was such a movement. The goal was New York. Boston and Philadelphia civilly refused to be interested in Western money, but New York was less coy, and politic young gentlemen in clothes from London or Brooks Brothers escorted daughters of mines and ranches to the horse shows or hastily explained to sons and brothers of ample Western ladies that nice women didn't go to see Anna Held, a girl of Polish origin whose carved shoulders and narcotic eyes informed schoolboys and their fathers nightly what a French courtesan would be like if she were facially able. Californian fruits and heiresses appeared seasonably in New York and were absorbed. It was assumed that all rich Westerners came wooing Eastern favour and since the Western cities were so crude and ugly it was not worth while to inspect them. To-day the Easterner slides in a motor past ranged villas in Pasadena and hears names of men who took leave to grow rich unnoticed by the *New York Herald*. He hears, too, legends of men who fantastically existed in this waste without Eastern noise: Henry, or Heinrich, Miller ran errands for his thousand cowboys in San Francisco and once was kindly tipped by one of them for his trouble. He heard that a discharged clerk threatened to shoot him and sent the man a silver-mounted revolver with a pink ribbon bowed on its trigger.

He shed tears on hearing that one of his favourite Poland sows was dead and a little later stood watching a drunken Mexican aim a rifle at his heart and lightly batted the muzzle aside with his hat, saying: "Do not be foolish," as the bullet killed a pony behind his shoulder. They told him how his compatriot Claus Spreckles had shocked men at a luncheon by saying that it was fine to be rich so that he could punish old enemies. Miller drawled: "I have no time to waste in having enemies," although he had certainly not been reading the verses of Emily Dickinson. He only once advertised himself in New York and then by an accident of taste. Miller got up during a performance of a silly play called "The Cowboy and the Lady," said "Chesus!" violently and stalked up an aisle muttering. Hundreds of soiled young men in rhapsodic hats would have told the New Yorkers that Miller could buy the theatre and burn it to express his disgust. No, his gross materialism did not lure the Easterner into this hidden world of opportunities and the midlander began to replace him as the banker of Western enterprise. Yet there had been a time when Bostonian merchants and chandlers came to lay aside their dignity, forgetting Stone Chapel and Brattle Street, and played the jolly faun in dance-halls of Dodge City, Cheyenne or Abilene. A tour through the West was rather the thing in the '70's. In the '90's sons of the tourists carelessly sold land bought by their fathers on advice of Mr. Ladd at Portland or Mr. Crocker at San Francisco for the price of an English drag in which their adorned wives were suitably reported watching polo at Westbury. In 1896 a silly beauty threw away her father's purchases outside Los Angeles against the advice of Joseph Choate. She and her urbane adviser are in dust. The land survives them, loaded with chromatic villas as the lawyer prophesied.

This altering society beyond the Mississippi begged for some great comedian to record its changes. But Owen Wister and Alfred Henry Lewis were busy with its past. Charles Lummis delved in New Mexico and Arizona. Kirk Munro told tales for boys. Mary Hallock Foote varied from sentimental romance to a sudden passage or two of bitter realism and critics neglected her to discuss something by Mrs. Humphry Ward or William Black. Stephen Crane flashed his short string of Western sketches through *McClure's* and the *Century*, refutations of melodrama in melodrama's terms. Doane Robinson and Vernall Webster seem to have vanished just as they began. The stencilled characters of Bret Harte returned thinly masked in the *Argonaut*, the *Wave* and the *Overland Monthly*. So in 1898 Harry Thurston Peck mourned: "I would give ten Mrs. Humphry Wards for one good, realistic novel about Denver or Seattle. Apparently Garland and this Edward"—he meant Edgar—"Howe are the only writers who take the West seriously. Crane's sketches are good as far as they go. . . . I am not slighting the writers whom you mention in your letter. They are all promising but they have not achieved anything so far—excepting Mr. Fernald—that warrants much excitement. The annoying feature of these stories is that the women are so badly studied. . . ." The critic saw the defect.

Women of the Western stories were feeble outlines. But women on dusty ranches of New Mexico chewed red petals and spat false blood so as to be sent in haste to the lighted verandas and Eastern voices of Colorado Springs. Women shrieked when a shot split the plain's belly and a grey bowel seemed to writhe as rattles clicked less loudly and the snake died in gracious coils. Women pressed on soiled glass, while men slept, to wait some train's far passage through tremendous night, moving to remembered waters that would not sink in summer and leave a mockery upon baked earth. Then there were women stately as great cows, and grammarless, before whose eyes the legend of the West had been erected. They had borne children on jolting floors of wagons, washed clothes that stunk from a week in oiled saddles and had piled salt on wounds in brown flesh ripped by bullets. They knew well just what happened when some drover's wife came from the East and a squaw vanished, richer, to her tribe leaving complimentary bronze offspring on the porch. These coarse memories gave them a drowsy smile that roused and glowed when they rocked in deep verandas among old men who quarrelled as to whether Pat Garret should have answered Billy the Kid's question, "Quien es?" when the lean marshal fired across the moonlit bed at Sumner and the outlaw died at last. They were likely to swear terribly if the champagne came too warm to table, and Art, for them, was just a lacquered bowl to be filled with litchi nuts for grandchildren or the gilded clock that so gently ticked out their time in a son's house beside the rocks at

93

Monterey. Perhaps the unforgotten kindness of their hands may raise them up a chronicler, else they are lost who were not ladies.

3

A very pretty lady went shopping with Frank Norris in Chinatown. The realist bought a pound of brown, dried fruits and puffed his breath into the bag as he strolled beside his friend, discussing San Francisco. The gaudy street was forgotten. He meditated: "Nobody seems to think out here. Don't you ever think it's hard to think in San Francisco?" But the bag exploded, just then, and the fruits rolled on the sloping walk. The lady laughed. Chinese babies ran giggling in blue silk to catch the spilled delights. Norris laughed, too, and they went away to dine in a room on Russian Hill and later watched lights of Berkeley spread as golden lace on the bay's farther shore.

Every abomination of building stood in San Francisco. Tourists shuddered and fled into the Silver Dollar to drink heavily, then stayed on Nob Hill's crest while tiny cars were hauled up the steepness below them on subterranean cables that still chuckle like contented ghouls. Islands stirred restlessly when mist fled over the great bay. The hills were tawdry gold in summer —dry grass on rosy clay—and jade in winter. On all these slopes things loved as homes reeled together in a drunken kiss and marvellous plaster roses hung on wooden doorways. Meaningless turrets sprouted from ledges of tin roof that descended toward Market Street's

uproar. None of this mattered. Crowds bawled at
prize-fights; crowds idled on the cliff while obliging seals
cavorted in a dazzle of spray on their theatrical rocks;
crowds splashed and yelled in the huge Sutro baths.
Old Joaquin Miller swore that he had to elbow through
crowds of poets in his favourite bar when he came to
town and lectured, with a white rose in his jacket, telling
ladies that "musicians will one day ransack the stores
of these Tartar and Indian musics for fresh rhythms
and measures." The crowd was king in San Francisco.
A sense of pleasure had been born here and here persisted,
somehow, in pulsing sunlight and iced shadow of the
streets. Sober Eastern æsthetes got enmeshed in the
chatter of the brown Bohemian club and are known to
have become frivolous among colours of its audacious
posters in which men were, obviously, men. The courtly
Ambrose Bierce once was seen escorting two magnificents
of literary New York to the scene of a good recent murder
and pointing out spots where blood had pooled. But he
himself declared that murders in San Francisco had lost
quality, and only a few killings of the '90's are memorable. If the high quality of slaughter had been maintained, Bierce would never have left San Francisco.

A friend printed "Tales of Soldiers and Civilians"
for Bierce in 1891 and the wit noted in a preface that
these stories had been declined by all the Eastern publishers. His art was candidly inhuman. The soldiers
and civilians are merely subjects of wit and destruction.
Character didn't interest the strange humorist, trained in
England by the second Thomas Hood. He erected his
mortuary filigrees with traceries from the style of Edgar

Poe and remarked to an amateur critic: "If it scares you to read that one imaginary person killed another, why not take up knitting instead of reading?" But he faced the secret softness of the general critic and only journalism paid his way in this world. The book of 1891 has three hundred pages. Private Carter Druse helps to kill his father on page 17. Peyton Farquhar's spine snaps on page 30. A mother's brains are bubbling from her shattered skull on page 52. Men die of fright on pages 90, 198, 237. About page 270 the ghost of a lady lacking the middle toe of her right foot disposes of her murderer. Death dances intricately. A seemingly dead woman revives and chews the ear of a panther as it bites a hole in her throat. A decaying Rebel corpse drives his own sword into a Northern officer's heart. Captain Coulter, half naked and blackened by smoke of his cannon, cowers over the body of his Southern wife slain by his aim. But once death's dilettante became human. "A Son of the Gods" is his tribute to courage. The prose breaks into phrases of stately excitement when the rider on the white horse gallops to death, as though the artist rose and cheered him on. For Bierce's valour was authentic as his wit. If it is true that they shot him against a wall in Mexico, some literate member of the firing-party heard a last pungency and the old man buttoned his coat and faced the rifles, smiling.

But the crowds are not to be seen in Bierce's few tales of San Francisco. Then Chester Bailey Fernald sent a Chinese baby trotting through the streets with an adored cat, One Two, for whom idols in a hidden temple underground were urged to provide another tail. The city was a vapour behind this distinguished godson of Rudyard Kipling. The infant became a citizen of the *Century* and so did Fernald's brainless, human sailors in salty yarns of genuine flavour. Mr. Fernald's talent engaged an audience and then he steered away into dubious seas of pallid social comedy, leaving admirers of "The Monkey That Never Was" and "The Spirit in the Pipe" sitting aghast. Plainly he read Kipling but his whole management was in another scale and at his best he was master of a chilly pathos hardly American. . . . The smiling city, though, had been just a backdrop in his theatre. The *Chap-book* appeared at Chicago, a symptom of a rash of little magazines. Suddenly San Francisco had the *Lark* well printed on tawny paper, edited by *Les Jeunes*. Gelett Burgess let his boneless homunculi, then called *Goups*, romp on margins of advertisements for coal and they peered gloomily around doors or swung over abysses in floorless rooms with a sinister dignity. They were not altogether domestic, then, and their father employed them in travesties of drear French art, those pictures of Eve in her old age borne along by prehistoric sons. Mr. Burgess produced an effect in black and white as a forecast of Masereel's fashionable effects now current. (The cleverness of the '90's was very much the cleverness of our moment. In the '90's you could agree with Charles Warner that the acting and singing of untrained Negroes was vivid and delightful. You could agree with Harry Peck that "the little grotesques of the comic supplement may one day be treasured and collected as types of a real art" and

97

the theme has supplied matter of ten essays in the year 1924.) If Mr. Burgess once or twice leaned on Rudyard Kipling, as in his "Ballad of the Effeminates," he was never much of a burden and he could juggle an idiocy with greater ease, perhaps, than any other humorist in verse save Guy Wetmore Carryl. He was abetted by Porter Garnett, who wrote a poem on Omar Khayyám that happens to be good and thus quite different from other such American poems. Bruce Porter contributed a graceful prose, characteristic as his shapely caravel for Robert Louis Stevenson in Portsmouth Square or his ventures in glass. Yone Noguchi's first verses were paraphrased. Ernest Peixotto designed covers. The magazine amused its readers and its owners for two years, then *Les Jeunes* signed its obituary on May 1, 1897, and the death certificate states that the *Lark* was born in a sunny studio far above the mingling vulgarities of the street. There it lived, a stranger to the crowd.

But crowds pile and their feet are heard in "Vandover and the Brute." Norris let his victim stand and ponder on them in the old Pavilion. They pass in noise outside the idler's windows while his pride collapses. They loiter and hurry in a constant being on Polk Street below the lair of McTeague. They pack close to the giant and his Trina in the smoky music-hall. An immense, common life appears and passes behind the bodies of the fool and his woman. Even the little girls who find Trina's smashed corpse trot in a chattering group. He could evoke a relentless sense of human movement around his sad comedians. And yet the city's robe of sunlight does not glow and there are no flowers at corners of the

98

tangling streets.   Only in "Blix" when the lovers idle
at sunset or laugh in a restaurant is San Francisco gay.
The moralist is there, beside the artist, and as health
failed, the moralist won in some hidden battle.   There
came "The Octopus," a tremendous melodrama with
Jehovah thundering at its close.   "The Pit" was worse.
The gambler in wheat and his tiresome wife run off to
begin life anew, the last prudent fluctuation of a moving
picture.   Cheap people were delighted.   This was comprehensible as "Uncle Tom's Cabin."   The artist had
become the bitter pamphleteer, still powerful, still adroit.
Yet he had never been partisan to his time's disease.
He had no duties in the politic club of reticent, tranquil
gentlemen who had quite excused themselves from seeing
God as a reckless satyr and seem to have chosen a side-
real lawn mower that smoothed landscapes for their
careful feet and paths among "old books that time has
criticized," comfortable topics, empty refinements all
forgotten, now.   At least he had been male.   But he
was not the poet of this city whose king of dandies sold
Mumm's champagne—the city that laughed when a
young athlete, a jeweller nowadays, led his own funeral
of cabs with himself for subject in the first wandering
vehicle.   Ugly, vulgar, adored in her wallow beside the
bay, she knows that her lovers return.   Poets are not
needed.

DEPRAVITY

THERE was a dinner at the Everett House in 1890 given
for a youth from Illinois who sat in awe across from
Elbert Hubbard's floating tie and hairs, beside Edgar
Saltus. Just one remark can be recovered from that
meal: someone mentioned Christianity and Saltus slowly
said: "Has it appeared in America?" The stylist was
beginning to drift from sight; his brother's death sad-
dened him; his first marriage was a failure; his best work
was done. He became a civil shadow. In 1913 a boy
was startled into rigour on hearing a man say graciously
in a doctor's antechamber: "I'm Mr. Edgar Saltus."
He lived to remark that America was the hypocrite of
nations and then he vanished.

The odd blending of smugness and hypocrisy with
which Northern editors treat all Southern affairs was
on hand in early spring of 1892. Spring blew from
the heating Gulf up Louisiana; African voices thrilled
in love's renewed excitements among fresh flowers; earth
seemed a body sweating perfumes, bared not ignobly to
the sun. This classic season was, for once, neglected
because a governor would be chosen in April and the
Lottery's candidate must be beaten at the polls. Northern reporters were appalled by the sight of gentlewomen
slaving relentlessly in committees. The legend of Southern ladies as languidly maudlin creatures was still in

force.   An occasion had brought Mrs. William Preston
Johnson out to head the women of superior New Orleans.
Edgar Farrar, Charles Parlange and Murphy Foster were
speaking—and rather carefully—of the State's wealth,
proving that the Lottery's annual dole to charities could
be excused along with the Lottery.   In its agony the
machine offered an income of a million and more dollars
to Louisiana for its safety.   Now the Lottery's real master was John Morris, an uninteresting gambler from New
York, who had foisted the thing on Louisiana, strongly
maintaining it through several fights; but the decoration
of the Lottery was General Beauregard, so adored by the
farmers of his race that one of them recommended Robert Lee as an estimable person, saying: "I hear Gen'ral
Beaur'gard speaks very well of him."   The lesser glory
of Jubal Early's assistance also belonged to the Lottery.
So the reformers walked carefully; in that atmosphere
of manners and sentiments they must be tactfully bold.

Congress had barred the mails to the Lottery in 1890,
but express companies carried its tickets everywhere and
paid its losses.   Even in Boston a revel broke out among
sophomores at Harvard when a lad won something in
1890.   In New Orleans people of many tints lounged
on corners, developing a set of superstitions in betting
and buying chances.   Did a fish seen in a dream mean
7 or 13?   The Lottery was indubitably a nuisance; it
drew idlers of all kinds into the city; Negroes wouldn't
work on farms up the river for days before a drawing,
and negroid legislators supported the Lottery in its difficulties with a solid loyalty. . . . General Beauregard's
position was one of candid sense.   He wasn't responsible

if fools chose to waste their time and money on tickets.
The reformers pled that the fools were an industrial annoyance. Most of the journals backed the Lottery.
The polite battle waxed and had its place on front pages
in the North—then lost the place.

Some wealthy ranchers, two of whom were certified as
literate by Harvard, decided to revive the obsolete practice of killing cattle-thieves in Wyoming without trial.
They were advised against this method of reform by the
veterans at Cheyenne who'd known Wild Bill Hickock
and could tell the real reason why Calamity Jane shot
Darling Bob McKay's sombrero from his head in 1872.
But the amateurs invaded Johnson County with force
and arms, twenty picked Texan cowboys who could shoot,
a box of dynamite and an English tourist anxious to see
this quaint, native pastime. Two lorn alleged thieves
were trapped at a far ranch and killed. Johnson County
then besieged the social critics, urging them to be hanged
for murder. Reporters came hurrying. After an awful
crash of journalism three troops of amused cavalrymen
rode down the olive turf from Cheyenne and took charge
of the amateurs, whose zeal was entirely spent. They
simply wished to be out of Johnson County for ever.
Californian earthquakes, floods on the Mississippi, the
rush of settlers into opened land of Oklahoma and South
Dakota, mixed with the end of this comedy in the news,
and Murphy Foster's election as governor of Louisiana
on April 18, 1892, was not much noticed. The reformers had done their uncomfortable work without appeals to the crucified Christ, blasphemous battle hymns
or any bloodshed not to be amended by a bandage and

some arnica. This phenomenon deserved attention and more compliments than it got. The Lottery went into exile without leaving its respectable defenders in the posture of criminals; the spring now had its due.

Our model of social movements in America is the freeing of the slaves by a process of religious excitements and abominable orations delivered in biblical rhythms with many quotations from sacred Jewish writings. The sincerity of both parties is never questioned. They enjoyed the human pleasure of calling each other criminals against the laws of God, tyrants, murderers, vandals and such other names as the recurrent megalomania of the primitive American suggested Delusions of grandeur overcame most of them. They invoked Christ with the freedom of mediæval kings in a brawl over the border. Realism began in 1861 with the usual spawning of profiteers and continued until Robert Lee's soldiers knelt in mud to hug his stirrups and Ulysses Grant gave the whole flock of triumphant valkyrs at the North a lesson in breeding. William Lloyd Garrison suspended the *Liberator* as his holy cause was now achieved. His admirers presented him with thirty thousand dollars. He went to Paris, as a good American should, and his son Wendell Phillips Garrison reports that his father's moral sensibilities were offended by the gory battle canvases at Versailles. But "he took real delight and lingered long in the art section of the Paris Exposition of 1867, of which he especially enjoyed the statuary where the intent was chaste." There is no report of his opinion on a marble group named *Soldat Americain Tuant Son Ennemi*. But the biblical rhythms and the uses of meg-

alomanics had been finely taught. Even George Augustus Sala could note that: "An oration with biblical quotations or phrases suggestive of the Bible's prose
is useful in stirring them [the Americans] as nothing
else would be. They have an uncultivated hunger for
pathetics." His last thought is from Sismondi. His
own thoughts are singularly scarce. The peculiar advantage of calling your opponent a transgressor against
God is manifest in the oratory of the Gilded Age. The
nineteenth century liked men to perform with voices and
hands, actors in a romantic tragedy, while discussing
economic and social issues. It wasn't until July of 1896
that a forgotten illustrator, Walter Appleton Clark,
dropped a journal showing the styles in oratory at
Chicago and proposed to a gathering of Bohemians in
Buchignani's café that all orators be strangled at birth.
He sent Buchignani from table to table with a long strip
of tissue and on this ballot thirty men voted for the
strangling of orators save one who scribbled: "Why
not boil them in oil?" Below that Jay Hambidge
wrote: "Too expensive," and drew a dynamically sym-
metrical coffin. This remote consideration might not
have been understood in the Coliseum at Chicago where
men would yell for half an hour after hearing an orator
melodiously shout: "You shall not press down upon
the brow of labour this crown of thorns—you shall not
crucify mankind upon a cross of gold!"

This uncultivated hunger for pathetics was easily fed.
On July 4, 1825, Charles Sprague stunned the Bostonians by telling them: "Where you now sit, circled by
all that adorns and embellishes civilized life, the rank

thistles nodded in the wind and the wild fox dug his hole unscared." If a eulogist of Sprague does not lie, many broke into tears and shouts of applause. This stuff was printed in schoolbooks; children learned and re-cited it. Then came Wendell Phillips, the summary of Mark Hanna's politician, a handsome man who liked to make speeches, the whip of the Abolitionists. He had not one-tenth of Garrison's honest ability and he was incapable of such a speech as Henry Ward Beecher's defence of the Union in England. The clergyman as-sumed that he was heard by reasoning men. Phillips simply made orations. He stated that God chained that age to the redemption of the slave. He wished to re-mark that Daniel Webster was dead, so he brought out: "The unhappy statesman, defeated, heart-broken, sleeps by the solemn waves of the Atlantic." All that was legitimate in his method is shown in his orations for woman's suffrage. His triumph was a discourse on Toussaint L'Ouverture, a superior Negro whose taste in dress was bad. Phillips concluded: "You think me a fanatic to-night, for you read history, not with your eyes, but with your prejudices. But fifty years hence, when truth gets a hearing, the Muse of History will put Phocion for the Greeks and Brutus for the Roman, Hampden for England, Fayette for France, choose Washington as the bright, consummate flower of our earlier civilization, and John Brown the ripe fruit of our noonday [thunders of applause]; then, dipping her pen in the sunlight, will write in the clear blue, above them all, the name of the soldier, the statesman, the martyr, **TOUSSAINT L'OUVERTURE.**" The Muse of History's duty was to be performed on December 14, 1911. This peroration also went into the schoolbooks. So in 1891 it was natural enough that a living woman presented Frances Willard to an audience thus: "One day an angel will take a pen of diamond and dip its point in the sun's chosen rays. Then she will write, high above the proud titles of Joan of Arc, Florence Nightingale and Lucretia Mott, the name of our loving sister in Christ's work who is with us this evening." The mingling of simple assertion with sacred names was somehow licensed. They had been reared in that school. Miss Willard thanked the speaker and began her talk "holding a lovely bouquet of lilacs and sweet peas in her left hand."

But an opposition was created. Perhaps there had always been an opposition among the minor folk who seem more interesting in their casual acts than do these paraded great. A generation was passing out of sight. There was the elder Henry James, once called the Chinese Mandarin for his ceremonious manners, who wouldn't surrender his emotions to Alfred Tennyson and calmly wrote that Emerson no more satisfied his mind than did chattering old women. John McClure Daniel hated the tawdry hotels of the '50's and pitched *Les Misérables* into his stove at Richmond. John Esten Cooke admired Villon before the English announced him. And now old George Boker came back to Philadelphia from his tour as minister in Turkey and Russia. He was still handsome, long and courtly. He still gave cheques to helpless young artists and still insistently read books in five languages. He was born in 1823. As a lad at

Princeton he awed the other children with his coats and
cravats, an appalling swell who gave suppers and quoted
Dante in Italian. Boker was just a gentleman with a
taste for verse, to be sure, but Lawrence Barrett revived
his "Francesca da Rimini" and again it was applauded
in England and America. The playwright came to New
York for a performance and faced the changing times.
A lady stalked up to him in the old Fifth Avenue Hotel
and ordered him to have the wine-cups removed from a
scene in his play. So he may have given some study to
social conditions in America. In 1889 he had guests at
dinner in Philadelphia and sat among them gracefully
railing at "the moujik orators who quote the Bible. . . .
In Russia they call them Village Christs." Then he contributed his mite against mythology, standing next day
on Chestnut Street in his Russian furs, twirling his white
moustaches. Petronius? Oh, Petronius was a second-
rate writer, interesting to people who fancied Sodom and
Gomorrha to be extinct communities. He lifted his hat
to his young friend, in the manner of his times, and
strolled away. He died in January of 1890.

Another astringent person went on with the opposition.
Charles Dana, editor of the New York Sun, sent a novice
to report Henry George. The boy was made imbecile
and covered paper with words of which he now recalls
only "lyrelike voice." This went into Dana's cell and
came out with the editor's comment over its face: "You
sound like Wendell Phillips reporting Saint John the
Baptist. I asked you to see a Mr. Henry George."
This was insufferable to a boy able to recite most of
"Toussaint L'Ouverture." Dana was lectured for some

minutes on style, composition and the beauties of eloquence, then the *Sun* lost a reporter. The rhapsodist
went hurrying for sympathy to the office of *Puck* and
showed Dana's cruel remark to Henry Cuyler Bunner.
But the humorist was curiously cool after reading the description of Henry George, and limited his sympathy to
saying: "Mr. Dana's wrong. I think it sounds like
Hall Caine." Bunner's aversion to Hall Caine was already public. There could be no justice in the frivolous
city. The profession of medicine had a recruit in the
next week; but the *Sun* continued its lancing of swollen
estimates. *Puck* mocked the politicians in its big, coloured cartoons that unkindly imitated the drawings of
Gustave Doré's illustrated Bible. So *Puck* and the
Sun were not wanted in conservative homes or in several
clubs of New York, Boston and Philadelphia. Yet
every club could take in the *New York Evening Post;*
Edwin Godkin's paper must be counted a member of the
opposition, for the editor objected to excesses of speech
just as he objected to cuspidors or to a defective Civil
Service.

Godkin once showed the weakness of American crit-
icism. He himself was English and his enemies called
him an imported snob. He had come to take wholly
American positions in many matters, though, and once
wrote an editorial in which Grover Cleveland was a
"Moses, leading the army of political righteousness."
It is to be supposed that this was just a figure and not an
appeal to piety. A fight began in the Woman's Christian
Temperance Union; the quarrel became publicly known.
The rebel accused the sacred leader of gross egoism, say-

ing: "In all her great work she has been but seeking a background for her personal exploits and a theatre for the exercise of her wonderful powers and accomplishments." A committee of four replied in words of Christian savour, telling the rebel that she had lost "the faith of her old comrades in her sincerity, the chaplet of their admiring love and the crown of leadership in the grandest body of women known in the world." The President's wonderful powers and accomplishments are admitted by the rebel as a matter of course; the Union, in crushing her, states with firmness that it is the grandest body of women known in the world. These insolences amused Godkin but he would not comment. "I suppose," he wrote to a friend, "that we must defer to these religious or semi-religious bodies in their overblown rhetoric." The position is plain: the civilized editor assumed that any body of speakers pleading what they called a religious or humane cause had the right of effrontery. He could be very tart to the Republicans for simply calling themselves "the Grand Old Party," without reference to the known world. Yet in the year of the quarrel among the Christian women, a religious gentlewoman, Rebecca Harding Davis, suddenly halted a young martyr in a meeting of early feminists by saying: "I don't see haloes over any of our heads, my dear."

Mrs. Davis had fallen badly out of step with the new school in social movement. She had no delusions of grandeur and she spoke of God in a pleasant fashion that was respectful without patronage. It had never impressed her that there was any crown of leadership to be seized. She saw that Edwin Booth had his Madeira and waffles when he came to dine with her in Philadelphia, and any guest could begin his dinner with a dose of whisky if he liked. In the early '90's a lad got remarkably drunk one night, smashed furniture in a brothel and spent some hours in jail. He found his mother's door technically locked in his face the next morning, and went to refuge with Mrs. Davis, who considered his disorders and said briskly: "Go up and take a bath while I get you some breakfast, you silly child!" She fed him and packed him off to young Richard in New York, with orders verbal that a job was to be found for him at once. In 1894 she was taken with pity for the wasted virgins on Cape Cod; so in February of 1895 the *Century* printed an essay, "In the Grey Cabins of New England," that no man of the time would have dared to write in such flat candour. She once gave a shock in Boston by remarking, before she was even married, that women desired men. She had noticed as much in her work among the labourers of mining towns. Now she did worse. . . . New England was full of decent girls who would grow old childless, morbid in a territory drained of men. It was all very well for Sarah Jewett and Mary Wilkins to write touchingly of them, but why in God's name didn't somebody do something for them? The Bostonians got up societies to improve the Russian lepers and to help the South take care of its Negroes. Here were these undedicate nuns at home. One clergyman had shipped thirty of them into barbaric Montana and they were easily married off. The West was full of cowboys and such things ready to assist in the production of babies.

She rather stressed the babies in her pleasant prose.

Frances Willard was appalled. The pretty old maid had passed her rhapsodic period. She now simply awaited the time to rejoin her mother in another sphere. Her father seems to have been less important in her thought. While waiting she still sometimes gave addresses in schools for girls and ended by shaking a finger at them and saying: "Be good, girls, be good!" The small son of one of her neighbours in Evanston, outside Chicago, once ran downstairs from some monster that was noisy under the bed as he got off his undershirt and appeared, aged eight, in the parlour before Miss Willard, dressed in mere tears. Miss Willard kindly begged his mother not to punish him, as he didn't know that he had done anything wrong. In that same parlour she once stood counting over the bouquets given to her at a public meeting. She must have dropped one in the train. Couldn't Ned just run down to the station and see if anybody had found it? Far away, in a house on Gramercy Park, the rather intolerant Stephen Crane was remarking that Miss Willard's affair with Miss Willard should be stopped by the police. In the autumn of 1897 she met Rebecca Harding Davis in New York, and told her gently that "membership in the greatest spiritual movement since our Saviour's time" should be enough for the virgins of New England. Mrs. Davis stood in silence that may have been rapture or penitence, or perhaps the words "You silly child!" formed behind her smile. In her old age at Marion she remarked to a caller that Miss Willard's views seemed somewhat extreme. . . . Miss Willard died in 1898. She was five years older than Friedrich Nietzsche, who wrote: "You have made danger your calling and in that is nothing contemptible. Now of your calling you perish." They shared the depravity of an extreme softness. The German rebounded from study of his own nature into exaggerations and harsh yells in praise of strength, building out of his weakness a philosophic concept of persistent honour. But thought was not the relentless pursuit of her own beliefs to Miss Willard. She accepted a formula and called on God to make it sacred. Her eventual vice was an enlargement of the weak clause, "Lead us not into temptation," and the civilization that she foresaw was a sterile meadow, dangerless, sprinkled with folk wearing white ribbons. She was, however, a pleasant person who excited devotion. One of her disciples used to get herself through crises of propaganda by pausing to say: "Help me, God or Frances E. Willard!" Help came from somewhere on the prayer and she resumed her work.

2

In a Christian country no book would be suppressed for quoting the eloquence of reformers at six congresses favouring purity held in the decade. Bits of this matter may be found in "The Encyclopædia of Social Reform," edited by William Dwight Porter Bliss, D.D. It is not recorded that S. Weir Mitchell, J. West Roosevelt, William James, William Graham Sumner or Arthur Hadley attended these meetings. Mitchell went to one session at Baltimore and remarked to a friend that he'd never seen people enjoy themselves so. There is no further interest in the business of stimulating purity.

Nor is there any interest in Anthony Comstock's life during the '90's. He began the decade by bullying a shopkeeper in New York over the photograph of a naked statue. In 1895 George Barrie issued a handsome edition of *Crimes Célèbres*, by Alexandre Dumas, lush with illustrations. Comstock was urged to take action, and a Catholic lady gave him the set of books, calling notice to the libels on the Borgias, on the nuns who had Urbain Grandier burned, and other lewd details of the rubbish. Comstock wrote a censure but did nothing. He then persecuted a fleshly novel of the empty Gabriele D'Annunzio, concurrently raising a row because dealers in athletic goods would exhibit the elastic breech clouts worn by boys playing football. These, he said, hadn't been worn when he was a boy in the country. He ended the decade by starting a fight over a photograph in "A Gunner Aboard the *Yankee*," in which seekers may find a naked sailor, less than half an inch long. His friends prevented a ridiculous disturbance. . . . In an able man such an obsession would be pathetic, as it saddens one to watch Thomas Rowlandson's decline. Hogarth's successor found it easy to draw trousers. Even in his lovely sketch of Angelo's fencing-school, there are seen traces of this mania. He dallied with knee ribbons, invented grandiose comedies of dropsied gentlemen. Gillray replaced him in caricature. By 1800 Rowlandson's soldiers and sailors were just handsome dolls ineffably trousered and skirts were becoming bifurcations. He rallied and fought hard; but an unfinished sketch is a mere trouser, a last luxury.

The flattery of the country-side appeared in America in the '40's. A noble farmer saves people of the wicked city in "Fashion." There followed a list of melodramas built with an eye to touring companies which would play them in rural opera houses. These shows included a pure farmer, a pure country girl, a villain from the city and an urban adventuress—that is, a woman in fine clothes who did evil that no good might come of it. There was also a silly old maid who chased all the men in the piece from the comic hired boy to the villain himself. She was or wasn't enjoyed by plain, unsought women watching her from leathern cushions in little theaters. The specific of these plays was simple: the country mice might have foibles or even stumble into sin but their hearts were in the right place. Much of the formula can be read in James Herne's plays, of which Clara Morris remarked that they had as much to do with New England as her corsets had with Eleanora Duse's hands, floating just then in "Camille," at the Fifth Avenue Theatre. . . . This was badly translated to Duse one night after she had thrilled the crowd by her scream, *"Armando mio!"* and people huddled into her dressing-room to gape at her, in a maroon wrapper, eating ice cream. The translation was ineffectual. Duse examined her hands slowly and said in bewilderment: *"Mais, je ne porte pas un corset sur mes mains!"* . . . Clara Morris was in the right of her assertion. "Shore Acres" was far the most honest of these plays.

Henry George liked it, after seeing Herne behave so abominably in "Margaret Fleming," a dreadful concern to the pure as in its last act a virtuous woman adopted her husband's bastard, which was quite improper and unwarranted. The rural drama made money splendidly from 1870 to the end of the century, and the whole formula was repeated in "Way Down East," the final glory of the school.

"Way Down East" is a demonstration in illusion, and it explains how Mr. George Moore's way was made cloudy in America. For Harry Thurston Peck liked "Way Down East." He admitted that the melodrama at the old Broadway Theatre was trash; but he went again and again to see the pure country girl tricked by a false marriage, and the polished seducer slapped by the gallant young farmer, and the snowstorm, and the comic fellow who sang his song about a woollen string to the air of a bawdy Yankee ballad of the whaling days. The apologist of Zola, Sudermann and Frank Norris was seen sitting thralled at matinées. It was an idyll of some kind. It enchanted him as did the suave graces of Mr. Moore's prose. His flirtation with the novelist went on from book to book. Peck telephoned friends in Yonkers, a suburb of New York, to announce "Evelyn Innes" in 1898 and wrote two reviews of the romance.

This extraordinary story will be incomprehensible to the next generation and it should be explained that people such as Sir Owen Asher once really walked and talked. Lingering specimens are to be found living among awed Americans in Paris or in liberal Taormina.

Sir Owen is an amateur of everything who undertakes to seduce Evelyn Innes, a pretty singer, by describing the philosophy of Omar Khayyám in parks and by telling her all about painting in the National Gallery, now a storehouse for the work of John Sargent, a fashionable artist of the '90's. Evelyn flies with him to Paris, where he explains Balzac's novels and cookery to her, then prepares to consummate the seduction by draping his frame in silk pyjamas and reading a bit of Théophile Gautier: "I am as pagan as Alkibiades or Phidias. I never gathered on Golgotha the flowers of the Passion, and the deep red stream which flowed from the side of the Crucified and made a red girdle round the world never bathed me in its tide. I believe earth to be as beautiful as heaven, and I think that precision of form is virtue." Evelyn puts up with this loon for some years; then her egoism discovers a pleasure in saving what she calls her soul and she goes into a convent.

Peck could enjoy Mr. Moore when he behaved in this way among drawing-rooms, smart restaurants and bars. But when the novelist led his rakehelly gallants out of London and chattered of lust beside hedges or in rustic houses, the critic couldn't stand it at all. He scolded Mr. Moore maternally in angry reviews; he called him the greatest—he used such words—the greatest novelist since Thackeray, but begged him to keep sin inside city limits, where it belonged. "My Lord, Harry," said John Kendrick Bangs, "are you this man's press agent?" Peck was. He helped Mr. Moore to become an idol of American writers who went meekly pattering after his diabolic shepherd's crook wreathed in orchids. They have not been able to imitate his delicate, running sentences that escape monotony by the turn of a word, a gull's whirl in the fog, but they learned about women from him.

There was no pure American country-side before the Civil War. Most of our coarse balladry dates from that time. The barbarous, dramatic "Frankie and Johnny" was known on the Mississippi in the '50's and was chanted by Federal troops besieging Vicksburg in 1863; a copy of twelve stanzas was made by a young officer and is preserved.* "Susie Skinner," "The Little Fat Dutchman" and others came from Puritan New England to the West in the covered wagons. These songs have now a name in the muff's slang of our moment. They are "pro-sexual"; that is to say that they admit the existence of lust among men and women, as candidly as do the ballads of any country. So the cowboys sang "My Lulu" and the soldiers in barracks on the plains put a wailing chorus to the impropriety, an air of the bugles:

"Bang away, bang away, bang away, bugle!
What you goin' to do when the bugler's dead an' gone?"

These collapses into biblical franchise are man's realism asserting itself against sentimental decorum, as Mark Twain once asserted himself when a living critic assailed Mr. Irving Bacheller for making mention of a man's navel in a pleasant story. Clemens lifted a white eyebrow and drowsily asked: "Haven't you got one?" There

* Mr. Emerson Hough dated this song from a murder at Natchez in the '40's.

were young boys in the room and the critic evaded a vulgar admission by changing the subject.

Clemens was of the superior rural class in Missouri. Manners of the inferior class amused an editor of Saint Louis in 1847. The rustics went to bed in the grand manner, then, even with a stranger in their midst: "the old man stripped unscrupulously and sought his share of the one collapsed-looking pillow, and the sons cavalierly followed his example, leaving the old woman, 'the gals, and the stranger to settle any question of delicacy that might arise." The risen question may be found in "The Drama in Pokerville"; the same volume contains a sketch that is simply an equivocation on an obscene word, and a true story, "The Death of Mike Fink," which has implications even less heartening to mythologists of a pure America. These books of the '40's were issued by a reputable firm in Philadelphia and were illustrated by Felix Darley, who in 1860 announced that he had never illustrated what he thought an immoral book. Obviously "Simon Suggs," "The Louisiana Swamp Doctor," "Yankee Yarns and Yankee Letters" were not held to be slanders on the countryfolk who gamble, brawl and carouse in their pages. They passed everywhere and are found stored in farm-houses. The young Wises, Staggs and Cabells grinned over them at Virginia Military Institute before they went out to be profusely shot in the holy war. Clemens read these adventures of pedlars and roaming preachers when he was a boy, and then in his gay winter of 1894 was frank as they were. He was amusing a crowd of men before the fire-place in The Players when Mr. Merritt Coulson asked him to criticize Henry Bunner's tale of a Northern Bishop rebuking the hysterical crowd at a Southern camp-meeting, "As One Having Authority," but the satirist refused to criticize and broke into jeers at the camp-meetings. His prudent mother never let him go near them, he said, and then told the story of a recruit in the Civil War unable to name his father, explaining: "Captain, sir, I guess I'm just a camp-meetin' baby." Mr. Coulson repeated this cynicism to John Hay, once Abraham Lincoln's secretary, in 1899. The diplomat chuckled and said: "Yes. Mr. Lincoln used to tell that one." In the same year a friend wrote to the diplomat apologizing for a song sung by an indiscreet young playwright at a dinner in Hay's honour. Hay answered in one of his short notes: "I heard that song when I was eight years old in Indiana. Yours, J. H. P. S.—He sang it badly.

After the Civil War the country-side began to purify itself in fiction and oratory. In 1891 its purity was extolled by a minor Populist speaker, Paul Suckow, who invaded New York and assured an audience in 14th Street that there was no such thing as impurity in Kansas. In 1896 the purity of the inner United States was proclaimed by both political parties jointly and severally. So some records of the year 1896 have been brought out, from the one reliable source, the notes of doctors in counties chosen because they were then wholly agricultural, without any taint of the industrialism which is supposed to breed corruptions. In central Massachusetts a young doctor began his practice in February. In the course of the year he was invited to prevent six illegitimate births. Two of the girls married. He attended the birth of one child, and knows nothing of the other cases. He notes that the youth of the town in which he lived seemed to believe that decorum was regional; they were models of virtue in South Duckleberry and went over to sin in Ethansville, ten miles away. The country then held less than four thousand people. There was one brothel in the county seat. In upper New York a county of some three thousand people produced six illegitimate children in 1896. The physician ends: "As I understand that this communication is to be anonymous I feel free to add that ten births occurred within six months of weddings. Drinking has always been heavy here and continues to be so." In central Ohio there had been a vice crusade, as they are now called, led by an Episcopal clergyman, and no known prostitutes were in his county. In 1896 there were eight illegitimate children born. As there had been only three such accidents in 1895, the doctors of the county came to terms with the reformers and the trulls were allowed to return. There was only one illegitimate child born in 1897. In Indiana, four illegitimate births and two births of children to wives by common law. In Illinois, in a county that held less than four thousand people, seven illegitimate births. To these statistics may be added an adventure of a young surgeon, afterwards distinguished as a military medical officer, who was benighted riding in upper Kansas in November of 1896. He turned into a farm-house and found himself charged two dollars for admission to a dance of young farmers and blowzy girls, the maidservants of the region. These dances were events of Sunday night, an aftermath of the day's propriety and a respite from all costume. . . . In 1917 at the head-quarters of a division recruited from the midland States, this same surgeon patiently talked to groups of pastors, eager women and, once, to three Catholic priests with an escort of laymen. The deputations had a common purpose: they wanted to prevent the prevention of crippling diseases among the soldiery, in the name of God. A bored young adjutant steered the callers into the brown shell of an office and sometimes stood listening to the talk, as the impersonal surgeon repeated that military necessity could not admit their interpretation of God's laws. In one group there was a thin, dark woman weathered by years on some farm, who began to rock as the colonel argued, and suddenly cried out: "Oh, you're trying to make our good boys just as bad as those boys from the city, but the Lord Jesus won't let you!" She became beautiful in the cry, a saint of the grand abolition in cheap blue silk. The Lord Jesus was a bearded man in a white robe out of the picture beside the melodeon in Sunday School, a name to be invoked against something hotly nameless in her blood that stirred under trees of her father's farm when she was young and a lad held her hand.

3

Paul du Chaillu stood with David Graham Phillips and another at the top of the steep front steps, still steep, of the Hotel Brevoort. The explorer had some skins of rare African monkeys over his arm and these wafted in the air of a warm spring night as he gesticulated. A

victoria came to the curb below through the mauve light
of lamps and Richard Harding Davis handed out a slim
gentility whose voice melancholy even in laughter enchanted that decade. The young celebrities came up the
treads; her glove was white on Davis's black sleeve.
Du Chaillu gazed and then stood on his toes to watch the
slimness move into the hall beside the tall man's shoulders. Couldn't one be presented? They nervously told
him that his conversation, flowing strangely between
two languages, might give offence. *"Quoi?"* the explorer gulped. *"Une actrice vierge?"* He lost his balance in the shock. An explorer, a realist, skins of monkeys and a spilth of cigarettes descended the steps rap-
idly in disorder and landed disparately on the sidewalk
of Fifth Avenue. *"Mais,"* said Du Chaillu, sitting up,
"I am yet *incrédule!"*

The Americans of the '90's achieved a frame of mind
that was apparent even to small boys; when the ladies
said "actress," they meant something else. Virtuous
women were driven over the downs of Nantucket Island
and pursued some harmless players who spent summers in
the village of Siasconset. They panted in lanes, bearing cameras, and asked children where the actresses lived.
Gaunt old Mrs. Gilbert, called Grandma in her world,
once whirled to snap: "Well, young woman, where did
you learn your manners?" at a large impertinence dog-
ging her black skirts. But the nation sat in gilded ul-
cerations of theaters and gaped at the women on the
other side of hot bulbs with speculation. The decade
became a little more liberal in conversation and in print.
Even that shy elf of Victorian writing, the word

"whore," came from its covert once or twice, rendered as "w——," which deceived nobody but gave everybody a sense of daring. Children were told that it stood for "where" and didn't believe it. This liberalism did not tend to realism. Translations of *Germinie Lacerteux* were failures and Stephen Crane's "Maggie" was almost a failure. Poor drabs faithfully presented were not what the Americans craved. It is unjust to say that Americans like sordid fiction. The parade of French antimilitarist novels, the ferocious *Biribi* and the *Sous Offs* of Lucien Descaves, were unheard of, save that one doctor of divinity who read French declaimed against *Sous Offs* from a smart pulpit in Boston. These *contes Zolatiques* offend the theory of Plotinus, which is sacred in America: vice must be shown adorned, thus inciting by its beauty to virtue, one perfection recalling the other. So the megalomaniacs sat and wondered about the pretty mimes whose names float in the memoirs of James Lauren Ford, and matrons would have been incredulous if they had known that the grand courtesan of New York—hence, of America—was a woman resembling an inferior cook, whose clothes were ordered for her because she had no taste. They saw her; she sometimes appeared on the stage. She was a Christian Scientist and suffered greatly from sciatica. Her charm was an exquisite voice that gave point to her humours, for it is sworn that she invented the phrase "a stuffed shirt," meaning a tremendous nobody. Her flat was jammed with facile, clever men when she gave suppers, the jaunty nothings who rolled dice for drinks in the old Metropôle, the writers of smart plays, cheap songs, forgotten reviews—pink Acton Davies, Paul Dresser, Clyde Fitch, who always seemed to lead his clothes into a room, and a luckless, charming man whose wife once crawled over the floor of their poor lodging in the pulsing woe of childbirth to open the door and find a messenger with roses and his card: "With love and loyalty, from Paul." But such a woman is not the courtesan desired by virtuous people, the seductress, she-who-lies-in-wait-for-husbands. The American cannot define vice but he wants a glitter; his delusion against realism craves that. He has been taught to believe in absolutes—grandeurs of lechery, prodigious wastes. So in the '90's his pastors heartily commended "The Sign of the Cross" with dark Corona Riccardo suitably undulating in gauze around a burly centurion in the midst of Nero's Rome, that suburb of the religious American mind where Nero exists as a purple obscenity leering from his box at edible white Christians on the sands below his perfected reputation.

Nero has always been popular among clergymen, to whom he represents the pure depravity; he did everything that he wished in the most expensive fashion. He began to be denounced in America along with the slaveholders. Bad historical painters of the nineteenth century enhanced him. Piloty showed him swaggering over ruins; Sigalon made him rather thin, scowling at a poisoned slave, a likeness of Mr. Calvin Coolidge; Siemeradski made him a point in a tumble of naked folk watching some Christians burn on flowery stakes. All these eulogies may be seen in a costly edition of Suetonius, issued by Gebbie of Philadelphia in 1889. The book sold amazingly; it is hardly expurgated. In 1890 came another edition of Suetonius, without a publisher's name, at one dollar, unexpurgated and illustrated by some Frenchman who admired Félicien Rops but who could not draw. Also in 1890 there is historical record of a parody on "Nearer, My God, to Thee," which begins: "Nero, my dog, has fleas." Novels representing Nero disagreeably were current, such as Dean Farrar's scholarly "Darkness and Dawn," probably the worst of his books. The emperor figured disgracefully in sermons; no pastor ever seems to have thought of saying: "This silly child." As only one-twentieth of the sermons annually delivered in the United States are printed, it may be assumed that some preacher once put in a word for the scared clown running in black streets while the soldiers yelled up a new emperor, whose servants begged his body from his enemies and spent two hundred thousand sesterces to burn it decently in the gold and white, not purple, robes he wore just last year at the feast of January. They were simple people, slaves and freedmen, and not literary. His old nurses and his first mistress carried the ashes to his family's tomb. If it hadn't been for all those trashy poets, they said, and his mother spoiling him so, why, he might have had a good, long reign and behaved himself. It is probable that they cried a good deal. But perfection of form is virtue, and the pastors carried out the instructions of Plotinus in the case of Nero. In 1892 a Reverend Earl J. Stimson circulated in the Middle West, lecturing, with magic lantern, on Nero "the Antichrist." A leaflet announcing his performance insists that "He will conclusively prove to you that Nero sank below the most degraded inhabitants of Sodom and Gomorrha. See Genesis XIX, 5." Dr. Stimson also had for sale copies of a work on harlotry, "The Maiden Tribute to Babylon," by William Stead. "The Sign of the Cross" followed. So there must have been an understanding nudge from elbow to elbow in December of 1896 when the president of Princeton told the undergraduates that Oscar Wilde was the vilest sinner since Nero.

An amateur of demonology has collected all the notes on Wilde published in the United States before the scandal. Unless there was a private cult of admirers in the country, Wilde cannot have been a great figure to Americans in the early '90's. His books sold badly and his plays were just successful, not triumphant runs such as "The Sign of the Cross" or "Shore Acres." But the same amateur discovers that Wilde was mentioned by clergymen in at least nine hundred known sermons between 1895 and 1900. His social position improved from Sabbath to Sabbath. He was "the king of England's intellectual circles" in Denver, Colorado, and sober parishioners of Cleveland heard that no banquet was complete without his presence. English Kings were his least companions in this eloquence. He condescended to Edward II and James I. He walked with the purple Cæsars. The crown of leadership in the grandest body of sinners known in the world could not be his; he had never thrown Christians to lions. One rector even seems to have read "The Picture of Dorian Gray" in his excitement; he produced Wilde as beautiful, rich and young. Pastors might have explored *Biribi*

or the milder *Sous Offs* and found that common prisoners and soldiers were not so remote from the dandy.   Or
they might have evoked from American legal or medical
print a tawdry fellowship of tramps, clerks in haber-
dashery, mere farmers.   A wretched schoolmistress of
the year 1894 was left where her jailers stowed her.
These vulgarians never followed the exquisite's shape
on Sunday.   He somehow was unique, a creature of perfumed alcoves, and Nero's house had a guest.   They
arranged a terrific setting around a simple medical fact,
and sinister music blew as this romance flowed along.
Trusting small boys asked their aunts why the pastor
talked so about Mr. Wilde, and one of them was told
that the poet ate babies, which was untrue.   The megalomaniac instinct had full play and Wilde's future audience was assured.   It even seems that cynical dealers in
pornography heard the tumult; in 1899 an agent was selling at twenty dollars among undergraduates a set of
photographs in a scarlet cover lettered, "The Sins of
Oscar Wilde."

A long freshman who looked over the photographs in
the spring of 1899 and naturally had read all Wilde's
work at once, was found guilty of sketching respectably
in the summer.   It was already believed that one-tenth
of an artist was something superior to a man of affairs.
The boy's father couldn't protect him; he went drearily
to Paris and in Paris stayed until his mother changed
her mind in the spring of 1900.   His stutter made him
shy; he loathed his task and spent most of his time in
such cafés as were haunted by Americans, ready to spend
his handsome allowance on food and drink for anybody

who understood the meaning of the word "biscuit."
Early in 1900 he was sitting with the *New York Herald*
and a bottle of white wine in what he remembers as the
Café de la Régence when a bleating voice asked:
"Have you a match?" The shabby, flabby face across
his round table was dusted with some yellow powder or
dried ointment on its brownish stains. Mr. Armstrong
shoved matches over the marble and the tall man began
to talk in slow, elaborate sentences, interrupting himself
to call for a glass as a waiter passed. The boy watched
his bottle empty itself and was amused enough to send
for another whose net content ebbed, diminished to nothing. Sometime during a third bottle a waiter dropped a
friend's card at his elbow with a scribble on the pasteboard: "That is Oscar Wilde." Of course the young
fellow blushed. Wilde instantly looked at his silver
watch, exclaimed at the hour and rose. Then his theatrical habit overcame him. He bowed and said: "I
remove the embarrassment," which wasn't quite civil after two bottles but may be excused as Art. The boy
was incredulous. No, that ugly lounger with a mouth
full of decayed teeth and cheap rings on his hands
wasn't the "yellow lord of hell's corruptions." Besides,
Wilde hadn't made an epigram. A few nights later he
found conviction in another café when Wilde came into
the place with a pair of simpering English lads, all very
drunk. He even made a sketch of the poet on the back
of a bill of fare. It isn't exhilarating. Still he wanted
to hear an epigram. One afternoon on the Pont de la
Tournelle he was pretending to paint the river in water
colour when he heard Wilde's voice in a duet with a

French voice, that of some middle-aged man who presently shook hands with the dandy and left him by the parapet. . . . The big youth struggled with a genuine fright. He saw a man, true enough, in bad, plain clothes. But the whole megalomaniac course of the nineteenth century was on trial, here, with its Masters, seraphs of æsthetics, great sinners and great wits; its abolitions of what it did not understand in the name of God now effected a miracle. He was afraid of this stricken posturer, the son of a silly woman who darkened her rooms and read verses to guests in light of candles so that her wrinkles wouldn't show. In a few years an older, more learned man would be addressing Wilde in the manner of that century as a fallen tower that once proudly shone in the sun's eye, a ruin fair for ghouls to batten on, a great silent talker making his bed in hell, and with other titles of Celtic endearment. The boy wanted to run when Wilde waved a hand and strolled up to him; but he might hear an epigram, so he stayed. He thinks that Wilde had been drinking; the voice was thick. The poet looked at his sketch and launched into a defence of formal art. Water could not be painted. The Greeks and the mediæval painters were right in showing waves as mere jags and curves of line. And then he aimed his cigarette at Notre Dame, purple in a sunless dusk, and hauled Old Paris from his historical bandbox. This river had rolled white corpses after Saint Bartholomew's Eve. Yonder had passed Catherine de Medici with her glittering maids of dishonour picking their way to mass among the dead. He turned out his elaborate imitation of Walter Pater's slow rhythms, and his audience was very badly bored. There is a phrase of our slang that will be forgotten too soon: "He did his stuff." Wilde did his stuff for the young fellow who wanted an epigram. The king Henry III minced along in a knot of slim gallants crusted with pearls. All the fripperies were on show. Mr. Armstrong softly stamped his cold feet and awaited that sparkle of words, something about something being more beautiful than the seven deadly sins, while the celebrated fribbles of the sixteenth century paraded. Then Wilde stopped sharply and rubbed his hands over his forehead. Was there not a spring in the State of—of Arkansas, very well recommended for rheumatism? Mr. Armstrong had heard of Hot Springs. Yes, that was the name. Wilde said something vague about fleeing like a wounded hart into Arkansas, and was silent. Mr. Armstrong's feet were icy and lamps brightened everywhere in the dim fronts along the river. But no epigram had come. Wilde sneezed suddenly and said: "Thank you for listening . . . I am much alone . . ." and the grace of that "much alone" is his best-remembered phrase. Then by an indirection he did a service to the boy. Mr. Armstrong wrote to his mother that he'd met Oscar Wilde, and was ordered home by cable within five minutes of his letter's coming.

On March 12th a doctor paid William James a compliment, calling his researches "great," and the psychologist turned on him, saying: "Great? I'm nothing but an asterisk!" Such reductions are horrible to the soft and to the inflated who would rather hear some man say elegantly and eloquently: "The unhappy statesman, defeated, heart-broken, sleeps by the solemn waves of the Atlantic," than be told that a politician is dead.

Wilde's art becomes too dusty. But he has his standing as a great sinner, and polite Frenchmen working in the vast cemetery above Paris show the way patiently when rapt Americans pant: *"Oo est le tawmbeau d'Oscar Wilde?"* This might amuse him in the hell to which his adorers have condemned him with full benefit of Clergy.

DEAR HARP

1

THE fancy of eternal damnation should be tenderly nursed by American writers on behalf of policemen who in general are dull, underpaid creatures and frequently fathers. As it appears that there are natures so feebly egoistic that they must be kept in order by an idea of God as an angry cat in wait for them beyond this being, the lot of the policemen should not be hardened by destroying the immoral support of a Babylonian myth. A decent casuistry should have prevented journalists of the last century's latter part from bragging that newspapers had made hell and purgatory ridiculous, hollow as the bragging was. For cartoons and ridicule have never damaged anything mainstayed by man's total unwillingness to separate the religious emotion from some ritual or from some set of legends. Artists of the Renascence mocked Saint Joseph, showing him as an angry cuckold scolding the stork in corners of pious scenes. Saint Joseph so comfortably survived the ridicule that in 1923 an American lady loitering beside his shrine in a French temple heard a decent woman address his idol thus: "Blessed Joseph, friend of the married, grant, if my husband is false to me, I may not know it or, if I find it out, that I may not give a damn" (*que je m'en fous*). She then tipped the saint one franc and went her way. Mysticism has its highly practical side; and the preservation of hell and purgatory is, at least, expedient until by a process of increased pay or by imposing uniforms the duties of policemen can be rendered alluring to the more intelligent. The calling may then be recommended to writers and other artists as likely to provide them with healthy exercises, worldly experience—which would be useful—and a social state of greater dignity than that at present in their power of achievement.

As the class to which William and Henry James belonged by birth sank from importance in the United States through its lack of courage, there was an alteration toward the religious standards of the other James brothers, Jesse and Frank, who intermittently attended church in Missouri between spells of brigandage and were accounted good Christians by their neighbours. In the mildly libertarian period that preceded the Civil War a gentle agnosticism had been plausibly prevalent among the civilized, and it was apparently possible to discuss religions in the drawing-rooms of New York or Boston in philosophic, not in emotional terms. Perhaps the slaughter of the young educated in the war impaired liberalism or perhaps the velocity of cheap evangelism, the apparitions of Dwight Moody and Frances Willard, made it less safe. Presently Robert Ingersoll was a lonely figure, roving the cities and dispensing the raw material of the eighteenth century's rationalism with a slab of tobacco in his pocket and a consummate sense of the showman's craft. Editors and critics, when he died, found it evasively easy to say of Ingersoll that he had given out nothing new, that his agnosticism—many called it atheism—was a simple derivative from Paine and Voltaire, but he more truly was a product of the Bostonian age, the tag end of an intellectual stir that died out in the rank commerce and collapsing dignity of the '70's and '80's. Among a people who mistake a shallow amenity for civilization, the profane lawyer was a little heroic, a solitary point of open protest, navigating in a void. Certainly there existed the body of thinking men for whom Mr. Irvin Cobb would at last find the name "innocent bystanders," but they preferred a voiceless peace to the humiliation recited in an unprinted letter to Mark Twain, in 1889. "A nice English boy came to dinner on Thursday. Carelessly said that he did not believe in the Virgin Birth. Every lady in the room jumped down his gullet and rent his garments from him." So in 1896 the thin Jeannette Gilder denied Stephen Crane's right to express his disgust with Hebraic wraiths in "Black Riders." It was timidly urged that free speech was any man's privilege. "Not if it hurts people's feelings," said the female critic; and the saying may be taken as the American's whole social posture before free thought at the century's ending. . . . Children of the '90's might hear religious discussion if they went idling in the haunts of the vulgar and displaced. There were cool, gloomy academies of sophisticated discourse up any alley in those days, deep livery stables where the voices of Negro hostlers mixed an oily languor with the harsh drawl of grooms as harness was polished on sunny afternoons; the adolescent of the succeeding time has found freedom in smells of gasoline and wayward gin; in the '90's freedom was perfumed with saddle-soap and leather, with rotted straw and dung.

But it was assumed that the Roman Catholics' feelings were not important enough to be spared, and through the '90's the sensitive American Catholic saw tippling, flirtatious choirs of monks on the stage in musical shows. "Notre Dame" could be made into a play without softening the lust of Claude Frollo for the gipsy girl. John Rockefeller and his crew were caricatured in *Life* as the Pope and a bevy of cardinals. The rather pretty parades and gesticulations of the sacred Catholic enchanters were already being aped in Protestant churches; but James Lane Allen could have his say on the isolation of a nun in the *Century*, and show his ignorance of nuns or their government. In 1894 the pastors were busy with Saint Bartholomew's Eve and the fabulous experiments of the Borgias in distilling. The Borgias, indeed, were almost Neronic in their popularity; Roderick Lazuoli's family offered such a compound blessing of bastardy, lechery and murder to the attacking mind that it was certain of an airing. In November of 1894 James, Cardinal Gibbons, poised some sugar over coffee of an agnostic guest in Baltimore and said with dry bitterness: "On my honour, there's not a drop of poison in the house."

Oddly the man who raised the pack against Rome in 1894 was a lean Irishman, Catholic and devout. He was a capable prosecuting attorney who gave his aid to a commission appointed by the Senate to examine the morals of New York City. This Lexow Committee began its sittings without the faith of the journals. How could a crowd of rural politicians cope with Tammany

Hall, entrenched in the affairs of New York for forty years, an undefeated organization? The journalists were cynical. But Mr. Goff was suddenly an uncanny prestidigitator in a dingy room thronged with reporters, evoking strange beasts from a bottomless hat. He summoned up Irish patrolmen who bullied contribution from bawds and gamblers, or took it from wretched immigrants in lawful business who assumed humbly that the Yankee police were like all police. The hog's share of this income passed upward from official glove to glove and vanished in a political haze over Tammany Hall. The scandal was superbly handled by the press; Harvey Scott sent a reporter hurrying clear from the misty slope of Portland to whip back news to the *Oregonian*. New York, the hussy, was taken in sin again! Irish names sprinkled the lists of outgoing steamers and one of these tourists died lately after thirty years of exile in Algiers. All the beauties of a moral reformation were now displayed. Brothels were dismantled; the vapid contents found lodging in the tenements and presently children along the Bowery were courteously guiding sailors and other students of womanhood up dirty stairs in the certainty of fees for each client thus brought in. The writhings of vice before the Lexow Committee had their place in the news all summer, even with the great strike gripping the midlands and Altgeld hardily pitching his epigrams at Cleveland. Violent Irish leaders of labour helped the fight along. The American Protective Association was suddenly in action on the broadest scale, complaining that the Irish were making America a Papal state, that priests were allowed to ride without paying on trains in California, that Irish aldermen had attempted to fund parochial schools from the treasuries of cities, that a statue of Marquette, the Jesuit explorer, was erected in the Capitol at Washington. . . . The campaign came on with every card in the hand of Republican orators. A dozen Democratic governments of middling cities were upset; in New York a fused party elected a forgotten reformer mayor; Theodore Roosevelt was appointed to clean the police and by this carom the apprentice harlequin came bouncing back from obscurity to the bright, noisy centre of things, where he remained until flags were lowered for him, and old Joseph Ignatius Constantine Clarke said amiably that the crooked Irish of New York had made Roosevelt great. So the Irish and their Church were rebuked, and then in the summer of 1895 the steamers brought home groomed, plump men from Paris in time to chaffer for paving contracts and the repairs of municipal buildings. Familiar faces showed once more in the saloons along Fourteenth Street or on the steps of Tammany Hall. The "boys" were back. . . . Their heavy voices laughed again among the chattering women whose sleeves that year were hams of pallid colour in the paddock at Saratoga or on the verandas of the vast hotels where the bands played Victor Herbert's newest airs and the composer, Samuel Lover's grandson, passed from group to group making his pretty speeches to the actresses and contractors in a queerly German accent. Richard Croker walked at his gorilla's trot, swinging his long arms, from horse to horse under the trees, and once appeared, as drags and victorias bowled in from the course, dumbly sitting beside a famous harlot in her English cart, so scared of her effulgence that his one remark was: "I think your check rein's too tight, ma'am."

Croker's bearded face had been planted on the Tammany tiger's bicoloured body in cartoons of 1894, and bets were made that he would leave the city after election. But he understood completely the worthlessness of the superior American in politics. Gentlemanly subscribers of the *Century*, the *Nation* and the *Arena* would never persist, effecting any permanent organized force. The fireworks of the virtuous triumph in November meant just another awkward period for the boys at the Hall, who must now get subtly to work through friends and go to the trouble of securing contracts from the city by stealth, while this reformer was in office. Croker endured in tranquillity and didn't seem to know that he was a beaten villain. One morning he strolled past awed pages into the high, sombre office of John McCall at the New York Life Insurance Company, wearing an odious purple necktie in honour of the financier. Perching on a deep leather chair, he fixed his unmeaning gaze on the ruddy president of this gigantic company and said: "McCall, I want you should lend Martin K. a hundred thousand dollars." McCall explained that his company wouldn't lend a gambling publican a hundred thousand dollars to build a hotel. Croker nodded and continued in his chair while wriggling Brazilian bankers, begging priests and agents filed to McCall's great desk. At intervals the lord of Tammany repeated simply: "McCall, I want you should lend Martin K. a hundred thousand dollars." The rules of a huge life insurance company were not his affair; he had pledged himself to find money for an ally, and a Democrat of Irish descent would provide it. All day he sat, contentedly immovable in his necktie, and at dusk the wearied financier telephoned frantically to a plunging banker, asking him to make the loan. Croker paddled down the marbles of the hallway beside a young attorney and said, with an approval: "That McCall, now, he's stubborn." He had been impressed. In 1899 he turned on the streets of Washington and pointed out McCall to an acquaintance, saying: "That's Jawn McCall, there," and adding: "He's stubborn." His peasant's intelligence could respect stubborn refusal. He had risen from an Irish slum by stubbornness and may have recognized the trait as worth a little praise. But too much stiffness ended in annoying him. He laid contribution on a theatrical manager of the '90's and was refused. Croker patiently wrote and sent messages for a month. Then snow fell heavily. . . . The gutter and sidewalk before the showman's theatre were not cleaned until incense was offered to the boss in Fourteenth Street. His rise had taught Croker that successful government in the American democracy is merely a vile exchange of favours, and his abiding offence is that he demonstrated the fact. His story has been cleverly manipulated by two sentimental journalists but he remains an obscure, grey figure in description. He was not unkind, not debauched or aggressive, yet he had no savour, and men who knew him long find nothing much to say of the chief. Other Irish leaders of his time have left legends; Croker was merely the ruler of New York and fond of handsome horses.

2

Sensitive Irish-Americans in 1894 suffered considerably and their recollections of the year are sour indeed. A puddling of social nastiness ran under the political fight. A gentlewoman whose name was Irish as Kelly was forced to take oath at a school not far from Ralph Waldo Emerson's grave that she was really Unitarian, as she had represented herself, before beginning to teach algebra to the young Yankees. Returning from this humiliation to her lodgings, she found a gang of Christian women rifling her trunk in search of a nun's veil or penitential emblems. In a middling city infected by golf a family whose wealth had enriched the town for two generations was nervously requested not to appear at the new golf club laid out on land donated to the game by the family itself! A committee of Titanesses had ruled against the admission of Catholics. There was a sudden show of the emerging American lady's will; two liberal young women rose against the brutality and there followed one of those guerrilla battles which no native author has ever dared to describe, a succession of calls and scenes, with embarrassed husbands and fathers lured in and out of the vulgar absurdity. Finally the daughters of light faced the principal Titaness and threatened to turn over the shabby facts to Democratic newspapers of the place. In New York a committee of females and pastors hunted down an intimate of Grover Cleveland and urged him to secure the president's approval of a bill excluding Catholics from West Point and Annapolis. These episodes were Eastern and the persecutors in all instances belonged to what is called respectable society in America.

Nonsense rioted for months, then slacked and was forgotten, no doubt, with the jokes of the year and its hats. There was even a public revulsion, after the election; editors gravely deprecated religious intolerance in America. Perhaps the Catholic advertiser and subscriber were already worth some conciliation or perhaps the incurable sentimentalism of the American editor was working yeast. In the latter '90's orders were given in offices of newspapers in New York, Cleveland and Chicago that no matter derisive of Catholics should be printed without strictest approval. That process of immunity began through which, in our day, a cardinal may issue pastoral letters against legislation, one priest may murder another in a drunken row or an archbishop may order the police to interrupt a lawful public assembly without more than the most passing comment in the press, while a Protestant pastor cannot be slaughtered beside his mistress, forge a cheque or manfully announce his retirement from belief in the miraculous birth of Christ without pages of condign publicity. Lately the city of New York offered this disparity in a public contrast; a melodrama centring on a rape committed by a Protestant missionary was played for hundreds of nights without objection; meanwhile a corporation announced that its version of *Notre Dame de Paris* had been suitably altered, "in deference to the religious feeling of thousands," so that Dom Claude's libidinous qualities were transferred to his brother. One lone review found the favouritism distressing.

There was no suspension of Protestant feeling against the Catholic in the '90's whatever the journals said. The published matter had fully informed pastors that their celibate rivals now commanded the largest audience in America, and the rest of the decade is spotted with underhand assaults of various Protestant groups on the ancient sect. The gospellers sank to methods which outdid those of the traditional Jesuit, as described by the smug English novelists of the century's middle. The quiet cardinal in Baltimore often had to act with speed to prevent some nuisance. Thus in 1898, as the nation lumbered sideways into war, with the heartiest approval of innumerable Christians who signed petitions for blood and sent them to William McKinley, Gibbons was denounced as an ally of Spain by a powerful Baptist preacher still alive. Simultaneously the same clergyman headed a mixed committee of Baptists and Methodists which appeared in Washington demanding that all Catholic chaplains be withdrawn from the battleships. Roosevelt sent the committee out of his office at the War Department with one sentence, but he then passed into his military incarnation and the committee hung about in Washington bragging too loudly of an ally in the President's Cabinet. So a Protestant attorney of the New York Life Insurance Company, which had strongly backed McKinley in 1896, was suddenly at the White House. The President instantly sent his promise to John McCall. The zealots pestered Abner McKinley and dodged to and fro around Mark Hanna strolling with his train of attentive gentlemen through the old Raleigh's lobby. They were still in Washington when the fleet sailed, armed with Catholic chaplains, and then withdrew, certain that Rome had set its hands on the President. . . . The attorney found a case of the Orvieto favoured by Leo XIII at his house outside New York with the stamps of a wine-dealer in Baltimore. James, Cardinal Gibbons resumed work on that dreadful preface to "The Collegians" which so dismayed his relative, James Huneker. In the autumn it was rumoured that priests were not admitted to the hospital tents at Camp Wikoff; one day a buzz passed under the brown canvas, through smells of typhoid, and the titular pastor of Santa Maria in Trastavere walked slowly down the line of cots, pausing to speak to a red-haired Unitarian youth of Celtic expression and bestowing a blessing which, he said, would do the boy no harm. He had been told that priests were being kept out of the place. It was a great relief to find that untrue. He sauntered on. . . . As this serene personage rose in power, a certain sort of noisy political priest was less heard of in America. The Church took on a higher polish, a more mundane seeming. Its banal buildings spread; its universities increased their scope, and instruction improved yearly. There was naturally a sharp yell of approval when the cardinal was vilified at a public meeting of pastors in favour of Prohibition in the month that followed his placid death. His writing was spiritless; he made no profession of deep scholarship and once unfortunately alluded to Christian slaves in Cleopatra's gilded barge; but his management was perfect and his manners might be effectively studied by his less politic and less interesting successors. . . . If his sect forsakes the dignified urbanity which protects it from hot satire now expended frankly on other areas of decayed Christian philosophy in America, all its vulnerable surfaces, its superstitions and inconsequences will be opened to rational attack, and its ancillary service to the police will be much impaired.

3

Dion Boucicault died at New York in 1890, leaving four hundred plays or adaptations and a false legend of himself as creating the gay, rollicking Irishman of the theatre. He did not. The comic Irishman existed in the English theatre of the eighteenth century already wheedling his master out of drink or cash and already saying "Be jabers." Boucicault merely took a competent playwright's licence of arranging this creature on the scale of Charles Lever and Gerald Griffin's tales. It has been forgotten that he made use of his own handsome person and musical brogue in "The Colleen Bawn," "The Shaughran" and the other variations on Griffin's "Collegians." Primitive theatrical reviewers in the United States saw clearly what he had done. Lever was still popular and Griffin's book had its day. Poe's famous curse on "London Assurance" is the only historical estimate of Boucicault in America, but obscure critics, when the Irishman was a figure in New York and Washington before the Civil War, took high exception to his Ireland and sometimes to his acting.

The playwright himself was shrewdly observant. When he returned to America in 1876 he found the Irish in an altered position and noted in a letter of 1877: "We are more popular in the theatre than ever. Young actors and singers commonly take Irish names for the benefit of the fashion. . . . In society a bitter prejudice has been stirred up by the unseemly conduct of some Irish political blacklegs and, I should judge, by the constant immigration of humble people from Ireland. Mark Twain has made great fun of some rich Irishmen for palming themselves off * as French and what not. I have no complaint to make of my own reception. My old friends have been kind indeed and Mrs. Leslie † tells me that I am the object of envy among the Thespians for being a social lion, although I am no such thing. But I have heard a great deal too much of humiliating slights put upon Irish ladies at balls and there are rules against us at one of the best clubs in town. The Emmetts, I believe, are the one Irish family who have entrée everywhere." He must have continued hearing a great deal too much of slights put upon Irish ladies through the '80's. A little before his death a young fellow complained that his wife had been ignored at some seaside colony. Boucicault said morosely: "Go West, my friend, and change your name."

This prejudiced social atmosphere with its religious draughts had not existed for the Irishmen who followed Thomas Addis Emmett into exile. They melted easily into the westward movements of the '30's and '40's,

* "The Gilded Age."
† A rather literary lady who attempted a salon.

shedding their habits from prairie to prairie so that families named O'Donnell, Connor and Delehanty are now discovered drowsing in Protestant pews of Texas and Kansas. The cultivated Irishman romantically disposed himself in a drapery of Thomas Moore's goods and found decent social lodging in New York, Baltimore and Washington. The phrase "a professional Irishman" had been invented before the Civil War, apparently in the music halls of New York. Then there was an intermediary period with the Irish clotting in Eastern slums, Fell's Point and the Five Points, "the ignorant, the poor, the uninstructed Irishmen" of Henry Ward Beecher's description. Just here, however, the theatrical forces, politicians, actors and songmakers, found out the commercial advantages of flattering this alien. Oakey Hall, that entertaining mayor of New York who spoke French in public and criticized Gustave Flaubert, appeared before the people on Saint Patrick's Day in a green coat and ordered the Irish flag run up over City Hall. Tony Pastor hitched an Irish verse to his ballad, "The Upper and Lower Ten Thousand," and Johnnie Pendy introduced one into "The Queen of the Cannibal Islands." Alice Somers, Maude de Lasco, Joe Hurley, Harry Duval and Lou Boshell had always an Irish song ready for the gallery at Pastor's or Niblo's. An Irish dance and song were tricks of the great travelling minstrel shows, Bryant's, Delehanty and Hengler's and Carter's Zouaves. Augustin Daly warily investigated Irish feeling through a friendly priest before offering Clara Morris in "Madeleine Morel" with its scene in a church's nave, and the actress's amusing memoirs tell how the company waited for hisses from the gallery of the '70's.

But while the whole parasitic class, dependent on herds for place in office or income, wooed the Irishman, native mechanics and clerks began to resent him; he underbid them at all turns; he would work for less and live in worse quarters. There was at least one anti-Catholic—implicitly anti-Irish—secret order in the '70's, the United Order of American Mechanics. The American Protective Association appeared in 1886, and in 1894 it was understood that there was a third. The cheaper professional Irishmen met all this parade of enmity with cries and allegations of wrongs done the race and the faith. But meanwhile the flattery continued with the abuse. The Irish were at once established as tremendously funny, gay and charming people and concurrently were snubbed. So there was turmoil at a literary dinner in 1896 when James Huneker contended that the Irish were seldom gay and his lonely supporter was Stephen Crane, who tried to make a difference between wit and gaiety, then brought on another broil by asserting that an Irishman could be a coward. He had now doubled Huneker's offence and the two were accused of abysmal affectation. This dummy figure of the Irishman had become deeply sacred with Americans; in 1898 a group of young journalists went hunting the first trooper to reach the blockhouse on San Juan Hill, assuring each other, said Acton Davies, that he would be a red-haired Irishman and warmly disappointed when he proved an ordinary American of German ancestry. . . .

Nineteen years later, another group of journalists went hunting a red-haired Irishman who fired the first shot of the American Expeditionary force in France. Some clever military commander will eventually sense an occasion and provide the necessary type.

The dummy of the '90's was an infinitely pugnacious, utterly common and merry animal, a fiction not yet done with, satisfying still to Americans who profess that they like an Irishman, and still know nothing about him. "Of all the tricks," George Bernard Shaw wrote in 1896, "which the Irish nation have played on the slow-witted Saxon, the most outrageous is the palming off on him of the imaginary Irishman of romance. The worst of it is that when a spurious type gets into literature, it strikes the imagination of boys and girls. They form themselves by playing up to it; and thus the unsubstantial fancies of the novelists and music-hall song-writers of one generation are apt to become the unpleasant and mischievous realities of the next." But in the United States, the natives, not the invading Celts, had produced the spurious type, and as the century ended, the American of Irish race was quietly, uncomfortably trying to escape his destiny. He had prospered dizzily in a hundred capacities, and now found himself classed, in most cities, as something unwanted outside his shop, his contractor's office or his bar. Under the green froth of Saint Patrick's Day oratory there floated sentences of expostulation. "We are good as the best of native Americans. Let them blame us for the acts of a few politicians and rioters and we will answer that for every Irish rogue we will find one born and bred under the

Stars and Stripes. . . . We can proudly boast that in every city in America where there is an Irish population are to be found cultured and dignified ladies and gentlemen." The strain rises, wistfully assertive, in the wearisome Irish and Catholic journals from which the clever writers inevitably vanished into offices of big newspapers.

The spokesman of the superior Irish in America had notably been John Boyle O'Reilly. He died only a few days before Dion Boucicault in 1890 but by the time that his mediocre monument was unveiled at Boston in 1896, there was little left of O'Reilly's reputation. He had met the American definition of a poet fully; ladies recited the vaguely radical stanzas of "In Bohemia" where recitation was encouraged and the pretty lyric of the roses was a legend on Christmas calendars, dusted with snowy mica and edged with shamrocks. "Moondyne," his Australian study, is now more active than his verse. A dozen unpretentious poets of the '90's outdid him— John Vance Cheney, Lizette Reese or, later, Arthur Colton. He had been a charming figure in Boston; he was honestly esteemed and his lectures kept the man's regal voice and manner in enough evidence to warrant reputation. There was no successor and throughout the '90's Irish letters in America were feebly represented by a few journalists, Katherine Conway, James Jeffrey Roche and the amusing Joseph Clarke who had his moment in 1898 when he replaced Henri Dumay as editor of the *Criterion*.

This mad review was founded by a retiring, gentle lady who somewhere discovered Dumay and brought him to New York. It was the association of a saint with a gambolling catamount. Dumay editorially pondered the intelligence of New York's social rulers and rhapsodized the little sanitary stops of a French dancer's dog. The young clever contributed in swarms. Perceval Pollard first was widely known through the *Criterion*. Rupert Hughes attacked the paper on its taste; Dumay noticed a good writer and engaged Mr. Hughes at once. His owner's interviews with the Frenchman became events and she finally paid the balance of his two years' salary to be rid of him. Clarke succeeded the roaming free lance, and the *Criterion* kept its tone of a French review of 1880 until the century ended and the magazine vanished into the leaden haze of the Decade of Muck. Like *Mlle. New York*, Vance Thompson's biweekly, the *Criterion* now has a devilish legend. It was engaging enough under Dumay and Clarke. Perceval Pollard and Rupert Hughes wrote soundly of books and music; why it was held "immoral" and refused by libraries is incomprehensible. But in those days it was also held eccentric for the artist, Alfred Brennan, to sign his letters with a French adverb, and a dinner of sculptors, all male, with erotic symbols in plaster on the table, has become one of the whispered orgies of Stanford White whereas the host and designer of the party was a sculptor who lived and died in a positive halo of marmoreal prettiness and domestic solidity. . . . Mr. Clarke was typical of these native Irish journalists; he had facility and a handsome breadth as an editorial writer; he dabbled in playmaking and versified fluently. He could not take O'Reilly's place, had he wished, and the '90's brought up no interpreter of the Irish in America.

A society which mistook amenity for civilization naturally had a low rôle for this untidy intrusion of people who spoke musical English and supposedly danced jigs. Pat and Mike held endless colloquies in the comic weeklies; the pig and goat watched through the shanty's door while a fat shrew belaboured her man with a skillet. The rich contractor and his wife strung with diamonds pushed at the social wall in cartoons and burlesques. A merry clown of the principal metropolitan court squawked across a dinner table to a lovely Miss Sullivan: "I suppose you're related to John L.?" meaning the prizefighter of the day, and this jape roused Joseph Choate, when he heard it, to saying: "We may think the Irish vulgar, but God knows what they think of us!" Perhaps it is safer to let the Irish speak, from the recollections of a man then young and always shrewd.

"My father and grandfather had been the best surgeons in X," says the deponent, "since the Mexican War. When I was a kid in the '80's, there were factories built and the edges of the city filled up with 'shanty Irish.' It never occurred to me, in those innocent days, that I was Irish. Father and mother both were born in America. He had the medical man's impatience of miraculous religions. My grandfather was a grand old warhorse of the Daniel O'Connell period, very courtly and gushing to the ladies. He always spoke of the immigrant millhands as 'bog trotters' and wondered why they did not take farms instead of working in the plants. . . . Everybody knew us in the city. It was about 1890 that trouble began for us. I was conscious of it as a boy is conscious that something is wrong. My sisters came

156

home from school in England and the beaux began to call. The oldest daughter engaged herself to the lad next door and then trouble really began. His family would not swallow any agreement that the presumptive children of this marriage should be raised in the faith. They were our warmest friends. My father secretly sympathized with them, I imagine. But my poor, devout mother was in the extremity of sorrow. . . . As a doctor I have had to see this situation played through over and over again, and until the Church takes a different position in the matter the Amerirish are always going to be in difficulties. The business ended in my sister and her boy eloping, much to father's amusement. She now attends a Unitarian Mosque in Boston. . . . I must describe Dr. Daniel O'D., the pastor of Saint Mary's. It is not my antipathy to formal religions but my memory of the priest that is speaking. Your soft-headed literary gang has invented a Catholic priest on its own pattern and doubtless he is satisfactory. Father Dan was a sour old prude, an educated peasant from South Ireland who had been a priest there before he came to the United States. He hated a Protestant and he despised Protestant education. Once he found me playing with some of my Nordic crowd on our street and told me: 'Remember, Owen, that you'll never see any of those lads in another world unless you should offend God and be sent to hell.' Of course the old man would go through ten blizzards to a death-bed or risk getting himself in the papers to beg a Catholic boy out of jail, and he got a hundred dollars a month out of my family for his poor. But I dreaded him, and his sermons in Lent scared me into a nervous misery although I was not in the least a sensitive child. You can find how he talked about hell and purgatory in Joyce's first novel. This godly man came to see that my people hunted my sister down and made her take all the proper Catholic steps. All our trouble came of being bad Catholics and bad Irishmen, he said emphatically, and too proud to associate with our own race. He was not at all subservient to wealth, I should say. I suppose he was entitled to his point of view. The Irish were the Irish to him. He had no use for American institutions of any kind. He continually denounced the public library in X for keeping books 'that speak against us.' His kind justified some of the A. P. A. twaddle. I do not suppose that there were many of them, but they did exist. He turned on me and said: "And here's Owen that never plays with any good Catholic boys!" . . . You pagans cannot understand a young Catholic's awe of a priest. This was not just a big man in a black vest speaking, but the Church. There is no good in trying to explain how this one sentence, just a slap at my mother underhand, drove me into Irish patriotism. I turned my twelve-year-old back on all my Protestant friends and associated exclusively with the Irish. . . . The Amerirish in X who come back fondly to me in memory were the middling kind. They lived in a little colony of frame houses on three parallel streets back of Saint Mary's. The men were superior mechanics or shopkeepers or little lawyers. The Nordics held them at arm's length and treated them in a half-humorous, half-condescending way, as the middle-class American treats the Catholic Irishman.

They had their defects, God knows! They were touchy and clannish and sentimental. Some of them flattered me for being the rich Dr. K.'s boy and some of them resented me tremendously. It is the weakness or the excessive sentiment of the Amerirish that no writer has spoken of that life in realistic terms. His book would be condemned and spat upon, but what an audience he would have! Well, 'the root is in their mother's heart and wrapped around their father's bones.' . . . Your literary fakers have neglected the extreme simplicity of the Irishwoman so as to talk blatherskite about 'Celtic poetry.' The Irishwoman born in Ireland is not gifted with much taste in dress or in household goods. I often think that the Amerirish girl develops into smartness and a fine sense of ornament because in her childhood she has to look at Mamma and the lithograph of His Holiness framed in bog oak on the parlour wall. . . . I can remember one of these good women saying to me in perfect sincerity: 'I wonder now why herself'—meaning my mother—'keeps the doctor's house so plain and him with all the money in God's world.' The men often had better taste than their wives, and the children differed from the young Nordics in very little, except that they knew those pure Americans looked down on them. Oh, yes, they did! Over on the edge of town was Irish Hill, where the 'bog trotters' lived, a stinking slum that started every epidemic in X and sold its votes to the dirty German politician who ran the Democratic machine in X. . . . Americans think in generalities. One Irish name equalled a Catholic and that equalled mud. Or if it was not Catholicism that was the bane, it was the social connotation of Irish Hill. Your anecdote of John McCall * illustrates the point. . . . A realistic writer about the nice Irish in X would have to harden his heart and transcribe such a scene as this. Here is young Terence stalking up and down the parlour with his chin quivering because those damn Republican kids at High School have gone and elected Robert Wilbur Abbott or Calvin Coolidge Jones captain of the baseball team and here he'd been on the team three years, and—and—and—— Over in the corner is Aunt Jane, who can remember O'Connell speaking at Cork, and the fine handsome man he was, telling Terry: 'Never mind, boy, them black perverts will find out in the next world!' The truth being that the Nordics were perfectly justified in electing Bob or Cal instead of Terry. As for pretty Norah crying her eyes out because she had not been asked to Sadie Smith's birthday party, I decline to discuss that at all. The worst of which was that the boys were frequently invited where the girls were not. . . .

"I do not deny that among these people, kind and well-meaning as they were, existed a lot of cheap Catholic bigotry and prejudice against the Nordics not on the grounds of their social superiority but simply as Protestants. You see I am talking a good deal, more than you like maybe, about the religious side of the business, because that seems to me the important thing in the

* A magnificent female at a dinner in Washington said to my father, across McCall: "He's not at all Irish, is he?" McCall asked her sweetly: "Did you expect me to bring a pig and a shillelagh with me?" She assured him: "Oh, dear no! I don't suppose you even keep a pig, do you?"

1890's. These people were often unconscious of their too frequent vulgarity and they attributed all snubs as relative to their religious nonsense. It was particularly true of the women, as they did not mix with the Nordics in business or wait on them in shops. I can remember women who themselves were shrewd and even witty who had manufactured a Protestant just as your critics have manufactured their chemical Catholic, who is a great liberal because he dislikes Prohibition and plays cards on Sunday. This atmosphere was frequently bad for the children. It was likely to make them flatterers of the Nordic for the sake of social advantages and it made many lads into toughs. They were going to show those Republican sissies how a real Irishman went on! So they hung around the houses of ill fame in the railroad district, got into fights on small provocation and thought it pretty smart to be arrested once or twice. I must take leave to say here that the attitude of the Protestant ladies in X toward these people simply struck me as implacably mean and silly. Well, God is for men, and religion for women, as Conrad said. . . . My mother gave dances a great deal and she kindly served as a social wedge for some of the nice Irish families. The boys all danced well. The girls were often lumps. For dancing was not approved of in some of those households. I know that sounds absurd, but it is true. My secretary at this moment is a pretty girl born in a small town of south Ireland whose family disapproves of dancing so much so that she and her brothers have invented a friend on whom they are calling at night when they want to go to a dance. Father Dan did not disapprove of dancing publicly, but he hated it and quarrelled over it with the other priest in X, a very progressive young American-born German. Why is it that only Theodore Dreiser and young FitzGerald seem to know that there is an enormous Catholic German constituency in America? And, oh, my, how the Amerirish in X looked down on them and snubbed them! Just as the other day I sewed up his head for a young Italamerican who had been try-ing to impress the haughty Harps on his street. 'They treat me and my sister like we was Polacks,' he said. For, putting Catholicism aside, the Irish can be awful snobs. I remember sitting in one house at X, and it was one of the most cultivated homes, too, listening to the family pore over the names of every prominent Irish personage in America, from Augustin Daly to John L. Sullivan. I hate to drag in that dead duck, the inferi-ority complex, but the root of it was there. And to-day I know Amerirish who would have colic if they read 'A Portrait of the Artist' or 'Ulysses' but who brag about James Joyce. . . . As to the virtues of these people, it strikes me that their generosity to their kids when they were prosperous was a lovable thing. Nobody, unless it is the prosperous Hebrew, is kinder to his children than an Ameririshman. It is more of a virtue, as they do not brag of it. Then, barring their noisy quarrels among themselves, they were and are mannerly folk. They like to please. Why not? It is a pity that they overdo the thing so often and get the name of flatterers. I remem-ber Frank Norris saying in 1899 that an Irish compli-ment landed like a falling house. There is also a basis for the rumour that Irishmen are witty. It is true that the most humourless creature in the world is a dull Irishman. The percentage of them is not small, either. Was not the humour of Dunne's Dooley papers the playing off of the stupid Hennessy against the sharp-witted Dooley? . . . When I was at college I knew two brothers, call them Dennis and Tom, the sons of a big Tammany contractor in New York, a terrible rascal and vulgar as a sewer. Dennis was immense. He had the cynicism of a French waiter at eighteen. He loathed his family. He despised Americans. He had an imaginary friend named Judkinson, a real-estate dealer in Brooklyn, who was the quintessence of American banality, an uncle of Mr. Sinclair Lewis's Babbitt. Denny was the first American I ever heard quote Bernard Shaw. There was a professional Irishman in our class. God permitted him to think himself a humorist and a gay dog among the women. He aspired to no less than Anna Held, who was the rage then. So he consulted Denny, as an expert in such things. Denny gave him the best of advice. Bill went down to New York and stepped up to the girl, as she was getting into a cab outside Weber and Fields', with a hundred-dollar bill wrapped around the stem of a rose. The girl tucked the rose into that feather boa she wore so much, then tore the bill into pieces and blew them in Bill's face. He came yelling murder to Denny, who looked him over and said: 'It's our national genius for treachery, you big fool, and do you think you'll ever be anything but Hundred Dollar Bill here until you graduate?' Bill could not stand being teased and left college, no loss to anybody. Your Yankee habit of automatically laughing at an Irish joke destroyed Bill. He had no more wit than his shoe, but he told jokes until the maddened bystanders ran from him. Just this morning I heard my young daughter telling a swain on the telephone: 'If you bring that funny Irishman back here, I'll have dad dissect him.' The boy was well enough except that he thought it his sacred duty to be funny. I remember when I was studying in Paris, an Amerirish boy fixing himself on Booth Tarkington one night in a café and driving him from table to table as he told him merry tales until Mr. Tarkington got wedged in a corner and could not run farther. He had the look of a man sitting beside his father's coffin, and I have waited for the episode to bob up in one of his stories. . . . Denny's young brother was in all ways his opposite. He was a splendid athlete, pious and dull as mud. But he was painfully sensitive about his father's reputation. He bristled whenever anybody said 'Tammany' or 'politician' in earshot of him. He suspected slights where none were intended, and thought himself unpopular when he was really admired. He changed his name, later, and lives in England, these days, avoiding Americans. As for Denny, he died at twenty-four in Paris. I helped the doctors take care of him. We were afraid to give him much morphine and once I tried to trick him with an injection of warm water. He grinned and whispered: 'National genius for treachery.' It was his contention that Shaw should have written 'genius for discovering treachery.' There were many Amerirish boys in college in my time, some of them good lads and well liked and some of them impossible. When these last were passed over in the elections of clubs and what not, they fell back on religious difference, or political prejudice. This 'black heart of Ireland,' is it anything but a lack of self-criticism? There was no religious prejudice at college and the young American is not politically excitable. . . . My own Scotch-sounding name and my agnosticism have always allowed me to hear what the Nordics think of the Celt without dilution. My Nordic wife malevolently insists that I stir the subject up. The Irish position in America has improved, of course, since I was a boy back in X. But what happened in X was the development of an Irish plutocracy against a larger Nordic plutocracy. Some of the best Irish families left X in order to be out of the social frost. One of those families changed its name. . . . That stunt was laughed at in the funny papers of those days but I have known intelligent Amerirish to do it with cold deliberation. 'What is the use,' one of them said to me, 'of having the children grow up with every damned matron on a hotel porch in summer-time lifting her nose at them because their name is Kelly?' . . . There were States in the 1890's where the Irish were better treated, such as California, where enough Irishmen had made themselves respected early to insure a kind of counterweight for the bosses and that amateur Robespierre whose name I forget just now, the Sand Lot man . . ." (Dennis Kearney, a popular leader, once very noisy). "I could say generally that the Irish were luckier where they were fewest and the Nordics had a chance to know them better. . . . As to American writing on the Irish, it has always been bad and is bad to-day. It either flatters them for possessing the ordinary virtues of decent people or it turns

them into comic supplements. Harold Frederic knew
a good deal about them but he used the common trick
of using their religious sincerity and nice manners as a
club on the Methodists. The rest of the writing in the
1890's struck me as just damned rot. There are some
clever sketches of Irish city types in O. Henry's things.
Dunne picked up his Dooley smartly, although I see no
overpowering humour in calling the Spanish prime minister a Spanish onion. I remember a writer named
Charles O'Keefe who did some grim little stories well
but there was not many of them." (Naturally: O'Keefe
died at the age of twenty-two.) "Such a writer as Seu-
mas McManus simply made capital of his background.
He was a mighty pleasant lecturer and told an Irish story
well. As for the professional Amerirish writers who go
around proving that a chief of police should not arrest a
fellow member of the Knights of Columbus and slobber-
ing about Catholic blood spilled on American fields, they
are simply *agents provocateurs* of the Ku Klux Klan.
Who ever heard of a Mason refusing to arrest another
Mason or a Presbyterian shedding tears on a platform
about Presbyterian blood shed in the Argonne? It is
against such slop that I wish some realistic writer, and
he would almost have to be an Irishman, would come up.
It is time for them to be done hunting poor compliments,
or treacheries either. Their muscle and their humours
are about all the Irish have really been allowed to show
in America. I love them too much to be patient of such
waste. So unless somebody else does it, I may hire a col-
laborator and do it myself. My life is well insured and
if the worst comes to the worst I can run to Hawaii when

they mob me, and cultivate pineapples on my plantation."

Yet the compliments, poor as they have been, perhaps came as a tribute from the writers who saw in this vain, charming, baffled folk a certain brotherhood to their own prosperous adversity, facing a society not "implacably mean and silly" but perpetually childish in its concepts of all art. They have flattered the Irish, surely, misting them in drear humours, drearier romances. But they stand in like case whose food is bought by the mere muscle of narration, an artisanship in gaiety, until the illusion of pleasure that supports all artists is sucked away and they see themselves as tired, as amused attendants in a glittering charnel where lamps shed no warmth.

THE UNHOLY HOST

THERE was a little revolt of one against the process of
education at Vanderbilt University in the spring of 1891.
The rebel was the son of a clergyman in Georgia, densely
shocked when a professor gave him translations from
Haeckel and a classmate advised him to read the perfumed insufficiency of Ernest Renan's life of Jesus. Rebellion carried him through a quarrel with a young instructor and into the office of the chancellor, a Virginian
gentleman named Landon Cabell Garland. The boy
stammered out expostulations; biology, agnosticism and
the sinfulness of the French language bubbled together
in his head and, being a Georgian, he had committed an
oration before the old mathematician said in his thin,
aged drawl: "Men never amount to much until they
outgrow their fathers' notions, sir." The rebellion of
1891 ended with the injection of that thought among
boiling prejudices. There came a stillness in Tennessee.
The boy mumbled something and stumbled out of the
room, whipped by twelve words from a drowsy magician
in a chair beside a window.

The chancellor vanished from his university and died
in 1895 just as Robert Grant told readers of *Scribner's
Magazine* that an American existed in self-righteous
commonness of spirit who sat at home in his shirt-sleeves,
reading the newspapers, and was "graceless, ascetic and

unimaginative in the name of God." Newspapers neglected Mr. Grant's discovery and printed very little about
Landon Cabell Garland. He had no "news value"—
Julian Ralph invented the phrase in 1892 although it
would be long before it became sacred. Improving journalism had won to a complete knowledge of its audience
at last and swept obliging rays across the form of John
L. Sullivan, whose neck was seventeen inches in circum-
ference, or dabbled the glory of a whole column on William Waldorf Astor, a man of means who fled the social
grossness of New York and wrote a number of tales to
celebrate his tenancy of an English castle. His tales are
now known only to eclectic amateurs. These "figures of
earth" were comprehensible, editors saw, to the graceless,
ascetic and unimaginative American. And what news
value had Landon Cabell Garland, born in 1810, celebrity in mathematics by 1840, professor of chemistry, as-
tronomy or any such sere art that needed teaching in the
South, president of a railroad in the war time and de-
fender of liberal education everywhere he passed? He
wasn't news value. Joseph Leidy, dying in 1891, the
foremost of American natural historians, stepfather of the
Smithsonian Institute, was not news value, but any
rogue who announced his faith in his mother's Bible and
his unaltered trust in the plain people whom he fleeced or
cajoled for votes was news value, and is to-day. The
notions of his father were sufficient to the graceless and
shirt-sleeved, in the name of God, and the passing of
that faint, scattered aristocracy spiritual which once dis-
turbed his complacency was not to be lamented. He had
his newspapers. The asceticism of growing dullness held

him to this fodder, and the arts abetted his feeding.

The arts, disguised as a young writer, now sardonically reminiscent, sat facing Edward Drinker Cope in the palæontologist's favourite restaurant, at Philadelphia. The arts were a little bored, listening to the strange, handsome Quaker debate a skull just sent from diggings in the West. Henry Fairfield Osborn had one opinion, Cope had another and the listening arts yawned into an empty glass, eventually so bored that they must ask Cope what was the good of palæontology? The professor fingered his jaunty waxed moustaches and began to simmer, then boiled over: "Friend, thee—you do not ask the poet to write bills of lading or the painter to whitewash fences. Do you expect the abstracted scientist to invent a patent churn?" He spoke, and presently the journals casually mentioned that he was dead, in 1897, in his house overflowing with papers and specimens of his long exploit in speculative history.

"In a way," says the man who insulted him, "I was excusable. Like most young Americans of that time I was all for art with a capital A, and I suppose my idea of a scientist was Thomas Alva Edison. The American idea of science was already so inæsthetic that Sinclair Lewis could have written 'Dr. Arrowsmith' with perfect propriety in 1897. Æsthetic, if you please, was an essay by Arthur Symons or a statue by Saint Gaudens. By the way, I am he who wrote to *Harper's* that the editors ought to be shot for printing Owen Wister's 'Em'ly' in the same number with Walter Pater's 'Apollo in Picardy.' Æsthetic, I repeat, was something graceful and smooth and so distinct that you didn't have to think about it

twice. Science was certainly not æsthetic. If Bertrand
Russell had called an Einstein of the period an 'explorer
in æsthetic' someone like Edmund Gosse would have
fairly cartooned him all over the magazines. I don't
suppose that people such as Cope cared a damn about
the neglect of their work by the critics and I don't suppose that Richard Swann Lull, Francis Tondorf, Edward
Maurer or Ellsworth Huntington care to-day what the
critics think of them. My sensation, when Professor
Cope flared up, was simply one of outrage that a grubber
among fossils should dare to put himself in the same
class with George Moore and Rudyard Kipling. . . .
Back of this disorderly theory of æsthetic I think you
will find the holy shade of James Russell Lowell. The
learned man of the golden '90's was someone like Lowell
who knew a great deal about all the right books and
talked about them gracefully. I choose Lowell as the
best of his kind, for you may tear him in pieces as much
as you like but you will have to admit his erudition
and his consistency of mind. Lowell, and his gang,
represented æsthetic. The Copes and Sumners and
Francis Amasa Walkers represented some dull nonsense about skeletons and wages and 'mores.' As far
as we were concerned they might just as well be trying
to invent patent churns as not. . . . I took Sumner's
course at New Haven, under protest, and, of course, I
respected him without knowing why I respected him.
He was a prodigious personality, something cold and
massive and autocratic. He came stalking into the
classroom with a sort of 'Be damned to you' air, and
even when he said something tremendously good he

drawled it out in his New Jersey whine with so little
emphasis that it wasted itself. I remember perfectly
his famous lecture on the expurgation of history, the
one in which he said that Ethan Allen probably did not
say: 'Open, in the name of the Continental Congress and
the great Jehovah' but did say: 'Open up here, you god-
damned son of a bitch!' But he never 'pointed up' his
good things as Barrett Wendell did and it was only years
afterward that I began to appreciate Sumner at all. I
find in my notes: 'When two religions appeared in the
primitive community the one favoured by respectable
cattle thieves was practised as religion and the other was
called illicit medicine or black magic' but that did not
impress me at the time and neither did his blistering dis-
courses on the crowd mind. He sat there in 1895 and
demonstrated the difference between morals and manners
as no American has demonstrated it before or since, and
whatever his biographer may say, he did shock his
students terrifically when he cut loose against protective
tariffs or pointed out that dress was the mother of
decency, not decency of dress. What was his subject,
after all, but this ape grown rusty at climbing who yet
feels himself to be a symbol and the frail representative
of Omnipotence in a place that is not home'? The old
fiend made it pretty plain that his opinion of the ape
was rather a low one, too, just as 'Folkways' shows you
what he thought of literature. We respected him, and
admired him, as I say, however little we appreciated
him. If he had been seriously threatened with expulsion
from Yale in 1899 when he blew up imperialism, there
would have been an academic revolution. His mind

may have been a little narrow, but he laid the foundations of social science in the United States and his neglect in the republic of letters, American department, has been shameful."

Dear sir, the republic of letters, in all its departments, can do nothing with a Sumner. He belongs on the high place over against the politic Jerusalem. It is said that from this windy eminence nations are seen as coloured sands poured carelessly through hands of inattentive demons and the haughty arts, themselves, viewed from above, are merely tiny emblems of man's protest against brevity and weakness, his poor revenge on God. This hill is no place for a good republican of letters, although now and then one steals off to join the unholy host around the accursed fires up there. But it is safer to sit discussing whether a sound style shouldn't resemble the running tone of conversation among civilized people —ourselves, in short. Our fathers' notions are warm around us. We do not care that, from the hill, we seem just lice, clinging to folds of a stale blanket.

2

Robert Louis Stevenson went not fully after the Lord as did Thomas his father, but wore a velvet coat, spent his shillings among venal girls and announced himself an atheist. While he was worrying his proud father remarkably in Edinburgh a quite commonplace farmer in middle Ohio asked the law to keep his only son from denying the regional god and spending his nights with a gallant widow of the Fourieriste persuasion.

The law replied: "This court cannot issue a frivolous order limiting any sane man in the free use of his faculties"; but the decision is possibly irrelevant in a case to be tried under the laws of the literary republic. Stevenson, then, rebelled and finally went the length of running away to California after a married woman whose husband courteously stepped from his corner of the forming triangle and walked off into legend.

Assuming the literary republican's viewpoint, all this is rather fearsome. As an episode under the laws of Ohio, or seen from the high place by Anatole France, there isn't much in it, except the good breeding of Mrs. Stevenson's first husband. The poet had used his faculties, for some years, as freely as his finances allowed. These practices were abhorrent to the odd, parochial Lord of Edinburgh, a creation something in the nature of an angry grocer, and even when his rebellion was done with, the poet never reconciled himself to the tartan bully.

His ample, light intelligence had been trained in the theatrical manners of decayed Calvinism, a version of the Christian philosophy which, in those days, excluded morality, the law of the individual, and dealt totally in manners, the laws of the herd. Stevenson had seen through this apparatus, but he could not discard it. His intellect was not legitimately rebellious at all, and the wistful apology of "The House of Eld" is the whole statement of his case. So the high place was not for him; but his levity impressed timid, bookish folk as red rashness, and for fourteen years a moving syrup of appreciation supported the gay invalid on its sweetness.

His subjects were inoffensive—murder and more murder, fratricidal hate and madness, blood lust and piracy in seven forms. His prose chimes gently on, delicately echoing a hundred classic musics, gently dwindles from the recollection as do all imitations, and is now impressive only to people who think that a good prose is written to be read aloud. But this theatre delighted the times: Vice and Virtue fought a duel in a frozen garden by candlelight, and Lord Rosebery was fascinated; the pirate ship sailed to a jolly tune and children watched the rain through nursery windows. . . . Only now and then an awkward sense of life intruded in the show, a sombre undertone welled up from somewhere and gave you Herrick, still disgraced in his own mind, staring at the white figurehead on the Presbyterian reef or the last paragraphs of "The Beach of Falesá," but generally the show was well in hand, one range of effects suited to peers and schoolboys and another conciliating the literary republicans: the castaway of "Falesá" will turn his talk into rhythmic prose or Herrick will score a phrase of the Fifth Symphony on the wall in Tahiti and scribble to his sweetheart: "Think of me at the last, here, on a bright beach, the sky and sea immoderately blue, and the great breakers roaring outside upon a barrier reef where a little isle sits, green with palms. . . ."

His decadence was just that of a man who has worked too hard in his apprenticeship and cannot escape from the schooling. Only it happened that this classical simulation was in high favour in the '80's, and that a hundred younger writers were pounding about among the *prosateurs* of the seventeenth and eighteenth centuries in search of some such medium for themselves. Hadn't George Saintsbury urged them to be *écrivains artistes?* Another set of decadents succeeded the humdrum, harmless people who aped Dickens and George Eliot, and Oscar Wilde appeared. The yellow and lavender carouse of the early '90's brought Stevenson into high relief. Good republicans saw that he was even more meritorious that he had seemed in the '80's. His name was suddenly invoked, as an image of chastity, against this terrible crew whose products agitated William Watson and scared the producers themselves. They advertised yesterday's mistress and to-morrow's satiety in verses wildly graceful as a painted Easter egg, and the whole business now suggests a college glee club rigorously intoning:

> "Gentleman rankers out on a spree,
> Damned from here to Eternity.
> God ha' mercy on such as we!
> Baa! Yah! Baa! . . ."

Some of these men were talented. Arthur Symons was a specimen of thermal conductivity in letters, through which the ideas of French artists passed into English perception with little damage. Lionel Johnson was an admirable critic up to the point of his rigid intellectual dishonesty. Aubrey Beardsley was a decorator so superior that his "Salomé" convinced people that Oscar Wilde had written a tragedy of the name, just as Oliver Herford's illustrations in some tales of the declining Joel Chandler Harris made American children of the '90's believe that they enjoyed "Aaron in the

Wildwoods" and "Little Mr. Thimblefinger." But the whole temper of the crowd was toward a species of languid exhibitionism that makes one grin.

"I cried for madder music and for stronger wine,
But when the feast is finished and the lamps expire,
Then falls thy shadow, Cynara! the night is thine;
And I am desolate and sick of an old passion,
    Yea, hungry for the lips of my desire;
I have been faithful to thee, Cynara! in my fashion. . . ."

The delaying melody charms for a second, and then the staleness of the phrases overcomes any pleasure in the orchestration. All this is still found momentous, by correct English criticism, and perhaps it is, if one can manage the straitly literary view. The audience rustled in embarrassment while the glee club sang. Biology was intruding in letters. Then the end came with a theatrical violence. Stevenson died in December of 1894; six months later Oscar Wilde was on trial for pæderasty in London. Some intolerable person announced that the dandy had made a new Thermopylæ of infamy; haberdashers in verse, men of fashion ran off to the Continent. Wilde blubbered as the crowd jeered him on his way to prison, and a voice came grimly out of Scotland: "How pure and clear our Stevenson's genius seems beside this 'art for art's sake' which the public now sees in its true colours at last!"

In the United States, the romancer had only one strong academic support up to his death. Brander Matthews had showed a limited enthusiasm, tempered by admissions of Stevenson's incurable Calvinism.

But for four years the English paraded in force. Stevenson was mourned honestly, sentimentally and politically by the right people: Edmund Gosse, James Barrie, Sidney Colvin, Ian Maclaren, Lord Rosebery, Conan Doyle, Anthony Hope, William Archer, Walter Raleigh, Arthur Pinero, William Watson and a number of forgotten greatnesses were all in print. The silences of Henry James, Rudyard Kipling, Thomas Hardy and George Meredith were nugatory, and George Moore's rudeness of 1886 was forgotten, if ever read. Under this manifestation the shapes of two acute publishers and an affable literary executor were dimly busy, and in the political eulogies the violet shadow of Oscar Wilde is amusingly visible, the more so that his name was never mentioned. The American result began to show in 1897, or showed itself to Harry Thurston Peck, Anthon professor of classical literature at Columbia College, editor of the *Bookman*. "I," he wrote, "am the last person in the world to deprecate poor Mr. Stevenson's posthumous vogue. He was a romantic writer of the greatest qualities, and while I cannot help preferring the realists, good romance gets under my skin very easily. But I cannot help feeling that these eulogies of Mr. Stevenson are going too far; and I greatly dislike the 'solar plexus jab' that I see in some of them, aimed not only at Wilde but at Messrs. Hardy, Moore and Kipling who all have burned a little incense at the altar of Aphrodite Pandemos, if you know who the lady is. For one, I am not sure that Mr. Stevenson's abstention from those tragedies and mishaps due to passionate influences in our human life was altogether the admirable trait that it is declared to be, by some of his friends. But then Mr. Barrett Wendell has rallied me on my 'morbid enthusiasm for amorous modern fiction' and I suppose that should put me in the corner where I belong. Furthermore, I dislike the personal element in much that is being written about Mr. Stevenson. It is natural that his friends should say the best for him, but why say anything of his 'pure, unsullied Scottish faith'? He was a free thinker, although not an atheist, in the manner of Mr. Howells and Mr. Crane. And why say that his life was an 'example to the young,' unless we are in for a very unexpected wave of liberalism in education? I have never heard that he indulged himself in stupid debaucheries but he was a gay blade in his green days and once was absolutely alienated from his father, who was of the unco guid description. How silly it would be to contemn Mr. Stevenson because he had a mistress or two in his youth, but how silly it is, on the other hand, to dress him up as Christian hero who ne'er brought the blush to maiden's cheek! I fear," the professor mused, "that his friends are overdoing it. . . . Well, I took your MS. to Mr. [James] O'Neill. He seemed interested in the subject and promised to read the play himself. He seems to be a shrewd, quick-witted man, and not half so conceited as I had been told by some of his acquaintances. My impressions of him are not worth a red cent because one of my toes was sore and Mr. O'Neill's little boy came and stood on it while we talked. . . ." *

But the stunning parade of the English grandees was

* His correspondent had dramatized "The Master of Ballantrae."

too much for the increasing type of academic instructor, forced into being by the expansion of the universities. In 1898 the flippant Guy Wetmore Carryl remarked that American colleges were the back yards of English criticism, and in 1898 two professorlings rounded on John Jay Chapman when the essayist attacked Stevenson as a derivative writer, quoting long paragraphs from Edmund Gosse and Walter Raleigh in their lectures. In 1899 the Vailima prayers were quoted at Princeton's theological seminary; and in 1900 the prose was introduced in five schools and colleges. . . . The comedy appeared in its fullest value to Mr. Charles Mason Maurice, an amateur who stuttered out his compliments to Stevenson at Saranac in 1888, adding those of his English teacher in a Chicago high school, and was answered gaily: "Eh, lad, I like your good word better. Professors are puir bodies when it comes to a tale."

Stevenson, here, is merely an emblem of the intellectual battle of the '90's in the United States. That battle, so far as it affected creative æsthetic, was won by the pack described in William Dean Howell's defence of "Maggie," those "many foolish people who cannot discriminate between the material and treatment in art, and think that beauty is inseparable from daintiness and prettiness . . ."; in the contemplative æsthetic of science and speculative history, the battle was an indeterminate muddle of fogged personalities, and in that haze the memorable beings of William Graham Sumner, William James and Barrett Wendell appear more clearly than the rest. But Wendell himself is rather an emblem than a man, vibrant point of protest against the vulgarization of American life, a realist in politics, a refugee among the dead in letters. He swayed before the dressed beef of his classroom and tried to illuminate it by chanting bars of the Elizabethan music in his amazing colonial English, or crackled with a wit that survives him: "Charles II was no more immoral than a cab-driver, or than some of yourselves, but his tastes were expensively administered unto and his loves were public as those of a fox terrier. . . . The modern theatre's only excuse is that it sends the milkman home in a good temper. . . . A writer in *Scribner's Magazine* tells us that good taste is universal in France. Good taste is not even universal in heaven." His method was not unlike that of little Arthur Wheeler, who faced the football-players of the Iron Age at Yale and lectured on European history, puncturing legends with a succession of groaning sniffs. . . . "Lord Nelson now arrived at Naples, where Lady Hamilton greeted him. Her experience of men was great and Nelson's intelligence was that"—sniff— "of a sailor. . . . Byron tore himself from the countess and set out for Greece. Even countesses become irksome and Byron had always understood"—sniff—"the advantages of combining his domestic mishaps with a little advertisement. . . . The Duke of Wellington, being" —sniff—"an Englishman, believed in letting his allies have a fair share of trouble in any undertaking. . . . If Napoleon's ambition to spread French culture in the Orient was reprehensible, that of the English to enlighten India has somehow escaped the attention of English"—sniff—"historians." But Wendell had the advantage of his topic: he was teaching "English

literature," his epigrams, his unconscious forays against
modernism, his saline comments on political affairs all
stood out in the tissue of the one subject popular with
the lazy undergraduate. Expanding universities now
offered ten courses in English literature to one in science,
and of this massive gift in cultivation about two-thirds
were devoted to the study of fiction. Thus the sopho-
more of 1900, and 1920, could pillow his brain on
"Treasure Island"; it had been conceded to his sloth
that he should not be vexed with "Manners and
Fashion" or asked to follow the lucidity of "Evidence as
to Man's Place in Nature"; it was certainly not suggested that the rich style of "Principles of Psychology"
was worth his while. These things belonged to "science." The beauties of fact became more and more
imperceptible, and the young poet who affronted Edward Cope was excused by an atmosphere in whose
slackened oxygen the duel of brothers by candlelight in
the frozen garden and the orchestral snivellings of
Tschaikowsky stood for perfected art.

3

Harry Thurston Peck was a Yankee gentleman whose
fractious brilliance as an undergraduate had startled the
little faculty of Columbia College. He was no friend
to strict accuracy, but it was early plain that he could
think, and in the middle '80's he began to write. He
wrote Tennysonian verses, a book for children, tabulated
the Semitic legends of creation, edited Latin grammars
and reviewed novels for the newspapers. In the '90's

his name, with its suggestion of frivolity, dodged here and there in magazines and journals. Columbia, itself, was regarded as somewhat libertine by other universities. It had no dominating religious tradition; it was assembled in godless New York; its professors appeared in smart restaurants, and published mundane "vignettes of Manhattan." The eccentricity of owning a professor named Hjalmar Hjorth Boyesen alone was considerable, and to have Professor Peck trace the permutations of "Ta-Ra-Ra-Boom De Ay" in a popular magazine utterly finished the place in the mind of one Bostonian educator, already unmercifully busy with the business of criticism.

Peck's interest in the world around him expressed itself anyhow. Everything took his eye—the life of street cars, the size of sleeves and the religious fervour of crowds attending unrehearsed ballets of football and baseball. He dashed off letters of twelve lines, as John Hay so often did, to tell an invalid friend in Colorado some anecdote. One learns that a tender young millionaire applied to Joseph Choate for counsel when a married woman was chasing him around Newport. "Tell her," said the lawyer; " 'Madam, I have no time for a liaison, but I am willing to oblige you, if you promise that our adultery is not to be of a serious nature.' " Or one sees the professor listening to a debate on the strike at Chicago among Mr. Henry Holt, Edwin Godkin and Richard Watson Gilder in a club, then listening to the same opinions from a group of workmen in a Sixth Avenue street car and so pondering: "It was very interesting, and the most amusing part of it was that a young fellow who was doing most of the talking looked so exactly like Godkin. Their grammar was awful, but they talked with great point and good sense. How much thought that we admire in the best magazines is commonplace to any sensible man, after all! Even the symbols and images that we admire in poetry are often but childish dreams and similes dressed up in a style." Or Stanford White had flung himself moodily into a group at Martin's, cursing softly and ordering white mint mixed with brandy, to soothe his discomfort when a great lady asked him to roof her ballroom in glass and silver. Or Brander Matthews had taken Peck to see a play, and how pretty Ida Conquest was in it! He added her to an imaginary seraglio inhabited by Clara Morris, Bijou Heron and Isabel Irving, "not one of whom," the professor added, "has ever met me, but has been respectfully adored from a safe distance." Things were not always so cheerful. Up came Sarah Grand's terrible novel, "The Heavenly Twins," which proved that there shouldn't be one law for men and another for women, and told how a girl went mad, contracting syphilis from a husband related to Ouida's guardsmen. The professor tried to talk of this book to some Western ladies who announced themselves suffragists and "They simply froze me alive. The woman's rights movement will never get along very far until women get down off the high horse and become rational in such matters. Mrs. Grand's book is important to their cause, and in stating their approval of her program, then refusing to argue the matter, they show the weakness of their repeated declaration of strict equality between the sexes. I often think that the

evasiveness of American women on such topics tends
to do harm to our young men. The boy who sniggers
and blushes when he is translating Catullus in the classroom must be the son of a prude. . . ." And the
devil tempted him to say in his essay on Grover Cleveland that the President had been accused of gross in-
decencies in his first campaign. Abusive letters poured
in on Peck for weeks after the essay was printed:
"Well, why shouldn't I have said so? The Republicans
called him a drunkard, a lecher, and I can remember
men who knew the addresses of all his illegitimate
children! Everybody knows of these vilifications.
Mrs. Cleveland must know of them and so does the
Cleveland cat, if there is one. Why leave that part of
the story out? What fools these mortals be!" The
devil tempted him yet again. He strolled up and down
a narrow drawing-room in lower Madison Avenue, ex-
pounding "The Songs of Bilitis" to a group of learned
ladies who nervously read some of the Lesbian biography
when Peck had left them, and then burned it in a
fire-place adorned with little crabs and stars in English
tile. They forgave him, and went in a fluttering clump
of cloaks edged with swansdown to see "The Sunken
Bell" when Charles Meltzer translated the heavy German fantasy and Edward Sothern played it, submit-
ting to this sadness for the professor's sake; he said it
would do them good. But mostly the world was cheerful around the cheerful man, supping with the De
Rezskés in their court of French parasites and jockeys,
with Charles Meltzer scolding the big Edouard for a
false note in "Faust." The establishment of the *Book-*

man gave him fresh importance. His taste kept the magazine from the pretentious heaviness that marked earlier literary reviews; in fact, there was nothing heavy about Peck. His coat had a flower; some of his waistcoats, even in the faded sheen of photographs, were illustrious of their kind. "Scholar, and wit, and something of a child."

In forty preserved letters, dated from 1889 to 1901, there are not half a dozen discussions of books. He sometimes made a little epitaph, or gave out an interesting portrait: "I liked Miss Woolson's stories better before she fell under the spell of Henry James. She was, by nature, a pleasing romantic writer of a sentimental turn. Her 'Horace Chase' is a funny mixture of realism and romance, but there are very good scenes in it. She caught the tone of masculine conversation very well. . . . Mr. James is impressed with her 'Dorothy,' I hear, through a mutual friend, as it is a theme that he means to tackle one of these days.* . . ." . . . "Henry George's funeral was most impressive. Poor people filed past the body for hours. He lay in state with his son's bust of him above the casket with several Catholic priests and ministers always there, standing close to the body. His obituaries have surprised me in their omissions. George was a humorist. He told a story splendidly and fairly sparkled with good things. He was not one of the sour, 'intense' radical brethren, but in all ways a genial, open-minded little man. He will be greatly missed in the socialistic world, although he had lost standing in recent years by refusing to embrace

* "The Wings of the Dove," perhaps?

communism as a long-lost brother. His single tax was enough for him; he never looked for a world where all our ambitions and impulses would be submitted to the will of our next-door neighbour. It was possible to disagree with Mr. George and yet to respect his disinterested goodness of heart. . . ." . . . "Yes, I sadly assent to your condemnation of the new Bangs book. The truth about [John Kendrick] Bangs is that he is not really a humorist at all. He is a cultivated, serious man who is at his best in little sketches of manners. He can write a pat review of any book and is very well read. But he began by writing humorous anecdotes and verses, and on he goes. There is always a sound idea in his things, but he stretches them out so that it irritates me, for one. . . ." "Mr. [Frank] Norris has taken a place with Doubleday, McClure. He is a most interesting personality, a silent, moody boy who never seems glum, although he can be obstreperous in an argument. He adores Zola, Stevenson, Kipling and the middle ages, the queerest combination imaginable. I think that you can see his feeling for Stevenson in 'Moran of the Lady Letty.' . . . He is a handsome fellow; his face suggests photographs of Hawthorne or of some classic actor.* Now why should you fall into the delusion of likening a man's character to his fiction? Is Ambrose Bierce a murderer because he writes about murders? Is Mr. James an infanticide because he wrote 'The Other House'? I never met a less blood-boultered

---

* "He was not exactly humourless but he didn't show much humour in conversation. . . . His face suggested an old-time tragedian . . . Edwin Booth, perhaps. . . . He had Booth's eyes. . . ."—*Jesse Lynch Williams.*

Banquo than poor little Mr. Crane. He is inoffensive
as a lamb, and Mr. Norris is extremely like him in
manner, albeit he has none, or too little, of Mr. Crane's
humour. The author of the terrible 'McTeague' is a
pleasant, cultivated young gentleman, inclined to be
obstreperous—and humourless—in arguments on realism,
but in every other respect a very pleasant boy. . . .
Your letter inclines me to the belief that there is not
too little imagination in the world but too much
of it. . . ."

His mind was a goldfish everlastingly drawn by some
bright object to glass of its tank, then swirling off in
fright to shelter in weeds. He had read a paper on
Nietzsche to a fugitive literary club in 1885 and ten
years later he began an acute, plausible description of the
heroic poet's content—then broke off on some interior
alarm and dismissed the madman to the mercy of God
in the ringing cant of a cheap evangelist. Ingersoll's
faded dialectic scared him. Howells must be scolded, a
little, for his pessimism. He looked with a quaint, wistful interest at the stout dogma of the Roman Church,
so secure among the changes and attritions of the
Protestant sects. You may watch the intelligence grap-
pling with some fiction, represented in the detached,
remote manner of the French realists whom he unconsciously adored. Ideas do not seem to shock him; he
surveys and describes the artist with the clarity of Edward Cope moving around a fossil monster; then the
Puritan drums beat all at once in his head and the
emotionalism of the American comes tumbling out in
undramatized, ridiculous sentences. His father's no-

tions triumph suddenly, and he frantically asserts the human dignity. There have been no evidences of man's place in nature; criticism ceases in a burst of frightened eloquence. George Moore must be slapped for his extrasphaltine adulteries. The huge indignations of Zola were preferable to Flaubert's cool suspension of identities. Immeasurably read, informed and shrewd, capable of much, he remained superstitious in the midst of his urbanities, and was at last ruined by a superstition —that wholly ignominious notion of his fathers, still earnestly maintained, that a man's sexual adventures disqualified his intellectual value.

There was, in the '90's a distinguished but scattering and, of course, ineffective effort toward a primary sophistication in American letters. Survivors of this movement, such as Vance Thompson, John Barry and the publisher of the *Chap Book* must have grinned, and James Huneker groaned aloud, when the new sophisticates of 1916 solemnly disclosed the works of Rimbaud, Laforgue, Vielé-Griffin and the designs of Toulouse-Lautrec, Forain and Cheret to a renovated public, when it was again decided that Felicien Rops had been overestimated, that Pierre Louys was merely beauty's ghoul and that Pierre Loti was a trifle thin. Wholesale thefts from Peck's paper on Stephane Mallarmé and quotations from Richard Hovey's translation of "Herodiade," without mention of Hovey, figured in the revival. Aline Gorren's study of Rimbaud was, naturally, not so much used as that of Arthur Symons. The process of recolonization, evident in the latter's '90's, implicitly established English critical prints as the best source of American critical writing. Even in 1925 it was possible for American essayists to approve a British essayist's approval of:

"We'll to the woods no more,
The laurels all are cut. . ."

without any mention of the obvious derivation of A. E. Housman's pretty lines. The triangular movement of the '50's, really, has been restored and the American habit of the '90's is cast aside. In the last decade of the nineteenth century there had been a very plain tendency, not at all unhealthy, to cut across the maternal intervention and to take ideas undiluted from Paris without awaiting the passage through an intermediary province. Peck's importance in the movement is plain.

In the summer of 1896 New York had a shortlived paper, *Tattle*, which roused enough attention to give an accidental impetus to the *Daily Tatler* published first on November 7th, by the young firm of Stone & Kimball. *Tattle* had given space to gossip about authors, during its brief run,* but it had mostly been news of courtesans, insinuating paragraphs on the mores of prizefighters and the like. Stone & Kimball's daily was quite literary, and placidly impertinent.

The *Daily Tatler* is good fun. The owners let it live for thirteen days, then killed it because it was too much trouble. People were amused by Edwin Emerson's

---

* *Tattle*, apparently, lasted from May until September. There is no file in the Congressional, New York or Boston libraries. It was on sale in New York and Chicago without a publisher's name. Names were not used at all, except in the sporting notes. It seems to have been a witless business, but it was extremely careful to keep within the laws. The number dated July 19th has an historic importance: the loathsome phrase "It's naughty but it's nice" occurs on the second page.

diary, in which the wit appears as Samuel Pepys, reborn, trying to ride a new "chariott made of two wheels," meeting Master Oliver Herford, Karl Bitter, Lincoln Steffens, David Gray, Samuel McClure at suppers, mistaking somebody at the horseshow for Master Gibson, the pamphleteering artist. The simulation of the Pepysian dialect is clever, and the trick pleased the times. John Barry's theatrical reviews inform you that "The Sign of the Cross," recommended by bishops and other theatrical reviewers, was a cheap affair, and that Maurice Barrymore was a poor actor. There is other evidence to this effect. James Barrie's arrival in New York is mentioned in a faintly sour manner, and irreverences multiply from page to page: "It was undoubtedly very wrong of Mr. Mosher to reprint Mr. [Andrew] Lang's little book. To print any book of Mr. Lang's is wrong, but to do it without paying Mr. Lang any money, or, more important still, any attention, is worse than wrong, it's discourteous." . . . "Sir Walter Besant, whom many people will remember as the author of a number of volumes, is writing a parlour play." . . . "Mr. J. B. Gilder's description of the Barrie dinner, to which he was one of the six invited guests (not including other reporters), is one of the nicest things we ever read. . . ."

But the unsigned verses are ruder than the prose. Here is Thomas Bailey Aldrich, adversely seen:

"Dandy Tommy, spick and span,
Struts before the Gilder clan.

All the Gilder clan bow down
To the beau of Boston town.

What though, like a lady's waist,
All his lines are overlaced?

What though, from a shallow brain,
Smooth inanities he strain?

In his emptiness content,
He achieves his ten per cent.

And secure in magazines,
Rules all rhymesters in their teens. . . ."

The Gilders seem to have been disliked in the office of
the *Daily Tatler,* for they appear five times in the thirteen numbers of the review. There are pasquinades on
George Woodberry, Brander Matthews, F. Hopkinson
Smith, and the rudenesses addressed to Elbert Hubbard
and to various publishers. But the general tone is amiable enough, even in an editorial discussion of the battle
in Boston, where an insipidly frivolous Bacchante by
MacMonnies had scandalized trustees of the Public Library, and the row satirized by Robert Grant in "The
Chippendales" was progressing. There are highly competent reviews of "The Country of the Pointed Firs,"
"The Cat and the Cherub," "The Other House,"
"George's Mother," "The Little Regiment" and a silly
depreciation of "A Shropshire Lad." You hear of forgotten monthlies, *Cosmopolis* and *Le Magazine International.* Richard and Henrietta Hovey talked of the
French poets. Many of Hovey's verses are printed, for
the first time, the fleetly famous "Barney M'Gee" among
them. George Barnard is civilly scolded for planting
fig leaves on his statues. Sadakichi Hartmann's unre-
membered "Tragedy in a New York Flat" is shudder-

ingly admired for its brutal realism. . . . There is too much about "brutal realism" in the *Daily Tatler*. . . . And Mr. Hartmann appears as a contributor in the next to the last number. Harry Thurston Peck is mentioned only once, as writing the whole contents of the *Bookman*. On November 10th the editors refused an article attacking Peck for his partial praise of Nietzsche, ending their rejection with a curious sentence: "We are the last people on earth to condemn Mr. Peck for his interest in European literature."

Peck's position may be judged through an autograph of a conventional female author of the period, perhaps too lately dead for mention here: "He takes," she reflected, "so much unnecessary trouble in dragging out the foreign writers." The true colonial spirit had revived in the lady, for she had once been something of an enthusiast for Tolstoy, Daudet and Turgeniev in the '80's when Howells, Henry James and Eugene Schuyler were making pleas for French and Russian fiction. But Peck had just rejected her poem on Robert Louis Stevenson, and possibly that had tinged her considerations of the professor.

He did drag out foreign authors, even some such as Petronius and Alkiphron who were not alive to trouble the colonial clique. Heathenish names sprinkled his casual reviews—Krafft-Ebing, Hugues Le Roux, De Joux, and in 1899 Remy de Gourmont, "a clever casuist." He was the first writer in English to describe George Moore with any sympathy and the first American who treated Huysmans, Mallarmé, Prevost, Sudermann and Hauptmann to more than a passing paragraph of uneasy regard. It is not a brilliant criticism, but it is alert and, until the Puritan ghost woke, levelly kind. His was the loudest voice in the forlorn group of American critics who took literature as something not inevitably conditioned by English opinion. His apostolate for Zola was continuous. He staggered a literary dinner of 1898 by saying: "Balzac, Shakespeare's equal and in psychology Shakespeare's superior," and later printed the opinion in *Munsey's Magazine*. His sudden heresies sent out ripples through one collection of literary autographs. Was there really an American who thought, in 1899, that another age would account the English scientists of the nineteenth century the strongest claim of English literature to remembrance? He said something of the kind, or was so understood in March of 1899. He, with Brander Matthews, Vance Thompson, Richard Hovey and the conjoint Stone & Kimball did what they could, in varying ways, for the European continent in letters. His reward was natural; in 1899 a sedulously Bostonian voice in the University of Chicago told a class of attentive students that they could not do worse than to follow Professor Peck's "garish" tastes.

He stands, then, in the muddle of the '90's as the superior American who wanted to be mundane, definitely sophisticated in the better sense, and who honestly strove to be liberal. Liberal he was, up to the point of admitting that a novelist might display the animal called man in the impartial mood of Huxley discussing crayfish. He could not attain a final position: ideas shocked him. Guy Wetmore Carryl's verbal epigram, "It takes two to make one seduction," distressed the apologist of Zola, so that he is remembered scolding the poet in a corner for half an hour. The urbane gentleman might become on any cross draught of emotion the lad in Wallingford, Connecticut, who cried over Longfellow's poems. The moralistic training had been too thorough. An idea was not, at the last, black ink on white paper, a thing to be dismissed with raillery. His demolition of Nordau took on the terms of an emotional flurry, sound as it was in its main contentions. He could perceive the social parable in Stephen Crane's "The Monster" where other critics, silly as the folk of Whilomville, saw only a "horrible" story, and he prophesied long glory for George Douglas when "The House with the Green Shutters" was issued in 1900. Douglas was already dead, but the professor did not know that, praising the boy's "resolute grip of situations that would be infinitely grotesque in the hands of a weaker writer." And yet it shocked him to hear young Carryl say that it needed two bodies to make one seduction! The obvious, to the end, could palsy this fine intelligence, even after he had come out as analytic champion of "Nana" and "Sappho" and had slung ice water on the range of English fiction, likening his adored Thackeray to a cynical old grandfather, calling the modern English novel a "bungling blotch of pruderies and false psychology" in a private letter of 1905 and at the same time issuing praises of Trollope, Tennyson and Longfellow. A hypocrite? No, he was an American.

After 1900 this mentality seems to divide itself. He rejoiced on paper over the worst "uplifting" novels of the calamitous decade between 1900 and 1910; students

eyed the flowered coat facing an unacademic prettiness
at luncheon in Claremont above the sweep of the Hudson and his classes were started by erotic witticisms
hardly gay while conservatives of the Columbian faculty
were dazed by Professor Peck's essays on perfumes and
the charm of women for men. Scandal flared; reporters
were sent hurrying among painted stuff of theatres for
notes on a strayed professor; in Cambridge an authority
recalled to his giggling sophomores that enthusiasm for
the light girls of Zola and Daudet; the graceless, ascetic
and unimaginative American was aware of Harry
Thurston Peck at last, a figure whirling in headlines
of the journals. "The crowd," said William Sumner,
"likes to see realistic representations of life, yet it also
likes to see in the drama that ridicule of the cultured
classes which seems like a victory over them." The
name of a dull farce, "Peck's Bad Boy," was useful to
merry folk of the newspapers. "Vice," said a person
in a pulpit, "has lured this brilliant man from the path
of truth." No definition of truth was supplied. The
triumph of his father's notions was complete, and a
crackling echo from poor lodgings in Connecticut came
as an anticlimax.

4

The dulcet Henry Adams, idling before his dead
wife's monument in the necropolis beyond Washington,
reflected much on the stagnation of the United States,
more and more ruled by crowds, desperately indifferent
to things spiritual. His mind was now preparing to

supply a false philosophic contour for history and some
critic not staggered by the historian's family name may
one day amuse us by showing how a man painfully de-
prived of a charming wife begins to discover the sex-
lessness of American literature, then becomes the chival-
rous rhapsodist of the mediæval Virgin. "The Education of Henry Adams" decorously omits the education
of Henry Adams, just as it describes the whisky of
shabby, provincial Adam Badeau and gracefully leaves
out the Scotch and soda flooding perpetually around
one of the proper friends so lovingly recited in the
languid, amiable prose. The Puritan aristocrat in this
much followed God: he dealt lightly with persons of
quality. The Count Cassini is the mannerly, if rather
unscrupulous, Russian minister, and never the ribald
commentator on American society who vanished from
Washington in a puff of lurid gossip under Theodore
Roosevelt. John Hay's triumph of 1901 is suitably
declared, the apparition of one's friend in the grand
rôle of international negotiator, but John Hay's poker
game with the English press in the spring of 1898,
with the sinking fund of the State Department as chips
at the little diplomat's elbow, is less memorable. One
learns that the sudden show of Germany in the Orient
threw England and the United States into accord, thus
gratifying a member of the Adams family extremely.
The decencies and moralities are all observed. The
world revolves in full dress around the reticent Bostonian, and the '90's make a fine show. You will idly
look down the index of the "Education" for such names
as Coxey, Altgeld, Garland, Bland. The machinery of

the comic opera in 1896 has no interest for the student of force. Mark Hanna is a shadow. William Jennings Bryan, the logical pendent of such figures as Charles Sumner and Wendell Phillips, has no existence, and the wisdom of the '90's apparently bored the idle witness. He gently regretted that he had never met Josiah Willard Gibbs, but he found Langley useful, conveniently located in Washington to answer questions while Professor Gibbs stayed in New Haven, at work. Psychology began to interest him and he makes us irritably aware that a department of psychology had developed at Harvard, but William James remains a dot in a group of professors, somewhere seen. Sociology occupied him, later, but William Sumner never came within his perceptual area. The education of Henry Adams was an exclusive affair, and magnificently futile. . . . One, having achieved impersonality without detachment, protested nothing, except the rudeness of John Randolph to one's ancestors. One did not mind the progressive cowardice of one's class. One observed the ugliness of chaos—chaos is always ugly to a moralist who demands rules, answers, codes and restrictions for his personal comfort. But the combative spirit of one's Puritan forbears had passed out of one, and one ended, with the rest of the Yankee hegemony, as a pleasing figurine on the intellectual shelf.

And yet to be a moralist, asking that humanity disentangle its unguessed motives and align itself to a program, a philosophic system, is not so bad as to go bawling in newspapers and magazines about the perils of the cigarette and bicycle for women, to spend ink in protesting French novels, the size of sleeves, the use of rouge. In discussing this minor morality—Sumner's "mores"—the literary republicans went a length to justify the sociologist's jeer: ". . . the literary products are nearest to the mores. . . . They lack all progress, or advance only temporarily from worse to better literary forms." The minor moralist is nothing but an item in the mores of his period; he records and perpetuates superstitions of the society which he dreads. It is impossible that he should stand aside from the social customs that surround him, take his two steps up the hill against Jerusalem and see, behind his moment, a long fluctuation of human absurdities, laws once sacred grown disreputable and tabus overthrown. He challenges no belief, imposes no new value on the human groups about him, and ends nowhere. He cannot be a realist, and he peculiarly hates that last turn of disillusioned romanticism which shows us stars flattened into tarnished tin, love yawning, ambition staled among its victories. So for the minor moralist of the aspiring decade that tried so hard to be purple, imperially grand, and ended in a compromised, ridiculous tint, there is no hope. He brought out a pale chatter in essays about "the temple of our American democracy," "the corruption of our financial life," "the falling ideals of our womanhood" and whatever he meant by all that is now too tedious for an attempt at discovery. The discussion of society is limited to a few papers of Howells, Robert Grant, Hamlin Garland and E. S. Martin who could assemble ideas and utter their protests in an intelligible prose. The theorists who followed the lovable Henry

George had, anyhow, a form and a belief. Elsewhere is vagueness and a rustling of waste paper. "Our social thinking," as Edwin Godkin said, "is growing more verbose and less dignified every day. . . ." In this void, naturally, the editors who had followed William Lloyd Garrison's habit of a personal tone came to profit and success: Godkin and Dana in the East, William Nelson and William Allen White in the midlands and Harvey Scott of the *Oregonian* were more and more admired. Editorials of superior provincial newspapers—the *Springfield Republican*, the *New Bedford Mercury*, the *Detroit Free Press*, the *Cincinnati Enquirer*—are quite as good as the solemn pettiness of essayists in the monthly magazines and the cultural reviews. Here, the American respect for journalism justifies itself; and the journalists, in varying shades of ability, did sometimes dare to flout "some great decorum, some fetish of a government, some ephemeral trade, or war, or man."

In this maze of intellectual timidities William Sumner emerges as a cold, ponderous groper, an Episcopal clergyman who threw off his silk and became deliberately an analyst of society, and the last libertarian of the nineteenth century in the United States. He was born so early in the century that he conceived the practice of free speech as an inalienable right of the American citizen, and education not as a species of social drill for the sons of pretentious women, but as education, an argument between the instructor and the instructed. His mind was essentially slow, unlike the flashing intelligence of William James; he wrote from first to last without grace or delicacy. In "Folkways" ideas are hidden around the bulk of a clumsy oratorical protasis and definitions must be exhumed as fossils from the marsh of swollen paragraphs. His mind freed itself slowly from conventions and inhibitions of his class, and that it never entirely freed itself is plain enough in his biography; but he took the one stride that separated him from other American sociologists of the period: he was able, finally, to assume an exterior view of all societies; and in the '90's the professor of political science at Yale College became a stormy identity on the edge of controversies, consulted by capitalists while he denounced their fetish, the protective tariff, quoted, without quotation points, in the feeble radical weeklies and journals while he openly preferred free capitalism to the paternalisms offered in some or another disguise. He had fought his way into authority, wrestling with the moralistic governors of Yale who dreaded his use of irreligious and rational texts; he would now fight anything from a bastard notion of currency to the government of the United States or, more powerful, the pruderies of a timid student. He appeared as the declared enemy of restrictive legislations, educational fig leaves and fluffy little white dogs, for which he had a distinguished aversion, as he had for anything frail, decorative and futile. He was the first real sociologist of his country, the first critic to protest the literature of financial success which, from 1870 onward, increased with the increasing vulgarity of the literate American, and the first American educator to approach the topic of decency without evasive words.

In 1897 his godson, William Sumner Dennison, who had never met the professor, came to New Haven and made his respectful call on this alarming sponsor. They got along smoothly for twenty minutes, and then the young doctor mentioned Mark Hanna, or rather the Mark Hanna then advertised by caricatures and libels. "Nonsense," the sociologist grumbled, "the first impulse in this country is always to lambaste a successful politician by calling him a dissipated man. It is the most effective method of blackening his reputation. You could attack his political ideas, but people have no thought about political ideas. They only understand a social personality—a man's manners or his vicious habits. Americans have no political ideas; they follow leaders who attract them or who know how to manage them. The kind of political leaders they like are human circuses." * He talked along. The American's stolidity came in question. Dr. Dennison was fresh from watching a revolution in South Africa. No, the professor objected, the new American was not stolid. He was emotional, shallowly emotional, easily whipped into an excitement. It took twenty years, he drawled, to start the Civil War, but the next great war could be started impromptu. He didn't like that. Emotionalism was "antisocial." . . . There seemed to be no growth of "independent thought" in the United States. The discussion of public events was puerile. When you had looked through the *North American Review* and the *Nation*, there was little else to read.

* This one sentence is synthesized from a letter written that evening, but the other statements, naturally, rely on Dr. Dennison's memory.

Oh, someone had given him an amusing book on "the tribal customs of children." He tossed William Allen White's "Court of Boyville" to his godson and then gravely dismissed his caller with a stiff old-fashioned bow.

Meanwhile the cheapening of the American was going on comfortably. The silly woman of 1892 who wanted the Populists tried for treason was now a general type. Altgeld and the Silver Knight had scared the conservatives. The mob was divided into two herds, both subscribing to the imbecile communism of herds. In 1899 the pompous idea of an American empire, with booted subalterns and barrack rooms, with ballads, in the Philippines, delighted journalists, and congressmen quoted "The White Man's Burden" in Washington. There was the usual fracas about moral duty which can always be used to cover a combined movement of interested politicians. Sumner roused, and then roared against this weary imitation of British imperialism. Followed the modern academic comedy; a pair of fatuous rich men in the corporation of Yale wanted the heretic shut up. But it was difficult to shut up a Sumner. The rumour of his expulsion came on. Two men of affairs charged eastward from San Francisco to protest. There was a twittering in other universities and a ripple of comment in the press, but Sumner remained intact and rumbling out objections to the flimsy legislations under Theodore Roosevelt which tried to correct the open coarseness of capitalistic method and thus drove it into subtleties. This legend of his expulsion is now firm among radicals and has been published, but he sur-

vived a situation that no professor could survive to-day
in universities where individualism is dreaded as nothing
else, wherein manufactures of patent drama, business
schools and courses for the propagation of fine em-
broidery are established on the order of the moneyed,
with professors shipped about as little white dogs in
wicker cells, the price marking the label. Sumner's
ghost was heard, for a moment in the spring of 1917,
when William Phelps shouted down the jeering boys
who had interrupted old David Jordan in a rambling
plea for peace, but the libertarian echo was perhaps the
last. What Richard Harding Davis protested long
ago in a romantic yarn has placidly happened, and
governors of universities fall into their natural place
behind the golden calf, bearing shovels.

Sumner is most articulate in "Folkways," the first
grand essay on the nature of human societies ever written
by an American but in many libraries left to the safety
of the "reserved" shelf so that young idealists need not
read the origins of cheap patriotism, the victimization
of man by his own clothes and customs. There is no
reason to call the attention of girls reared on "The Court-
ship of Miles Standish" to a gross form of Puritan wooing called "bundling." . . . This mind, immense and
clumsy, with traces of the moralist, moved in his last text
to regions uncomfortable for the merely literary and his
synthesis has no standing among critics, save as a source
of unmarked quotation. The book is a ghost. . . .
Sumner himself seemed a little ghostly in his last years,
a bulky, stern figure moving in heavy robes of an academic procession, or listening in the rear of a huge

lecture hall while Richard Lull chivalrously deplored the extinction of the sabre-toothed tiger and the amiable little eohippus, or described the strange domesticity of the amœba. Indeed, the old man seemed most at home in dim, high spaces of that museum where man is but one form of many that live and have lived, where beasts stuffed and strung on wires are ranged to show another age what once stirred and drew its breath in freedom.

THE AMERICAN MAGAZINES

SLIM, often ailing, wrapped in gay, soft robes, Egeria used to sit beside these windows, above the quiet little park. . . . The long room seems modern, unlike the taste of the '90's? Yes, but this hard, white paint was laid on in 1887 by a workman whom Napoléon Sarony found for Egeria's husband. There is Sarony's photograph of Egeria behind the seven-branched candlestick. But of course women used to crop their hair in those days! Nothing is newfangled; the fashion was called *la recluse* and you can see it in old albums of French actresses. No, the great candlestick was not bought yesterday in Grand Street. Once, in the brutal winter of 1882, when New York's slums were flooded with Jewish families, refugees from Russia, Egeria and her mother were shopping on Fourteenth Street, in falling snow, and a woman big with child lurched against the girl's sealskin cloak, then slipped down on the iced pavement while her rabble of frightened children tried to lift her and a bearded father groaned. Egeria's mother made out with her few words of Russian that they had no home, no food, no hope. She packed the tribe into the coupé and loaded them off to a private hospital, cashing a cheque, in passing, at the Fifth Avenue Hotel. . . . A while later there was a grand dinner, here, and old John Skidmore was exchanging thunderous witticisms with Mayo Hazeltine of the

Sun, when the butler stooped at Egeria's shoulder to whisper that a Miss Lazarus was in the library, "a very odd-looking person," and the girl came up to see a pallid woman curiously shrouded in dull, red velvet. The father of the rescued family, said Emma Lazarus, was a brassworker, and this candlestick was his first making in the new country, an offering to the benefactress. "May it light great happiness in this house," the poet said, and lifted her hands for a moment, and went away.

The room is modern, if you like. In the '90's ladies deplored the Russian trinkets and Hungarian embroideries. It was "eccentric" and not French, or "cosy." The Negro in the silver frame? That is Edward Gill, a tenor who sang in drawing-rooms of liberal people. He was a fad of 1892 and 1893. Edouard de Rezské ordered him to Paris for training, but he vanished, and his patrons never knew what became of him. Alfred Brennan did the little sketch. Brennan? He was Joseph Pennell's rival, and only Mr. Pennell has praised him since he died. You'll find a good deal of his work in the *Century*. He sketched himself for Egeria and signed the picture, "A. B. *ætat* 600 from being an artist in America." . . . Oh, yes, they used to talk so, even back in 1895! Poets and story-tellers stamped up and down this room, cursing the magazines by which they had to live, and asked questions about Paris. Wasn't it cheaper to live, over there? And that atmosphere, didn't your mind work more freely in it? And, and—— The chryselephantine image beckoned and they raised hands to test the wind toward exile.

The black-eyed woman in the oval frame? That is Scalchi. She sang here, often, and her fees must always be presented in bunches of Parma violets. Underneath her is Henry Cuyler Bunner, the editor of *Puck* until he died in 1896 and Harry Leon Wilson succeeded him. You'll find his "Short Sixes" in the bookcase. Yes, it was he who wrote:

> "It was an old, old, old lady
> And a boy who was half past three . . ."

A humorist who sinks into sentiment sinks very deeply. Think what Mark Twain did to Jeanne D'Arc. . . . Those are some of the correspondents in Cuba, on July 3, 1898. That is Frank Norris leaning on the tree. That's Richard Harding Davis shaving over the bucket. The man without a shirt may be Ralph Paine or Arthur Lee; they looked alike. Yes, Frank Norris came here, once, with his pretty wife. Egeria thought him charming, and not humourless at all. You'll find the suppressed first issue of "McTeague" in the bookcase, with that reference to little August's personal moisture. . . . No, the bearded man is not Joseph Conrad, although the likeness is staggering. That is Wright Prescott Edgerton, the military mathematician, who spent ten years craftily digging in mazes of red tape to humanize West Point and had the pleasure of hearing a president of the United States take the credit of his endless work. He was the son-in-law of Mrs. William Tod Helmuth, the famous doctor's wife, a primordial suffragist who once told Joseph Choate in Paris: "You see that I can pick the winning horse at the Grand Prix, and order a dinner so as to satisfy even you, and take my children all over Europe without a servant or a courier, but I can't vote and your illiterate coachman can!" There is Joseph Conrad, across the room, in the faded snapshot. Brede Place, Sussex, September of 1899. That is Moreton Frewen with his hat under his arm beside Mrs. Stephen Crane. Yes, the man in gaiters is Henry James. After the photograph was taken Egeria and Conrad strolled out into the country, talking in French. She admired some passage—she forgets which one—in "The Nigger of the Narcissus." That must have taken effort? The dark little man shrugged and tossed his glass into his eye. "Ah, madame, we are always so much praised for things that we do without thinking and the really difficult affairs are passed over!" He agreed with her that the high art of fiction was to find a detachment. It was not necessary to be inhuman, or mocking, but a detachment was necessary. What else had Flaubert, Anatole France, Stendhal and Turgeniev? Dostoyevsky? Oh, that amateur! She was slightly shocked.

The other snapshot? That is Guy Wetmore Carryl whose variations on La Fontaine in *Harper's* amused everybody. He was a good deal dreaded for his tongue, but Egeria thinks he was a soft-hearted boy enough. He came, hysterically white, and stood, there, at the fire-place, cursing the magazines that wouldn't buy his story of a young rake in Paris, ready for suicide, but relieved by news of his rich father's death in barbarous America. He stood and raved. But, said Egeria, filling one of the green cups with kümmel, did you expect them to buy a realism? Carryl banged his hands suddenly on the mantelshelf and said: "I'll make it worse and make 'em buy it!" You will find it in his volume of Parisian sketches, neatly dressed out in the formula of Robert Louis Stevenson. The Americans of the '90's were discovering that you can tell any story if you tell it lightly. . . . Yes, the slaves of the magazines came here, and raved, and sometimes put their heads among the trinkets of the mantel and wept. Egeria reached for the kümmel in its purple flask, or for the chequebook in the rosewood table, as there might be a wife in Brooklyn, or up in Harlem. . . . Look in the big tulipwood box with silver handles. These are all literary autographs. What have you there? . . . "Of course the magazines will print stories by Rudyard Kipling about horizontal women and locomotor ataxia, but if an American tries——" Put it back, and don't read the signature. That refrain gets monotonous in this, and in another huge collection. What's that? . . . "My natural disgust with your American public which so ardently supports the fiction of Mr. Hardy and ——" Be discreet! Never look at a grandee in his undress, especially when he seems to be talking of money. His published opinions on commercial writers are those that we must believe. He was a little annoyed to see that *Scribner's* would make a serial of George Meredith's "The Amazing Marriage" and that Hardy's "Jude the Obscure" was running in *Harper's*. Authors should never write letters without a friend watching the pen. . . . But see how gracefully Mary Wilkins answered a congratulation on "Jane Field" when it was a serial in

215

Harper's in 1892. And Owen Wister, you see, depre-
cates Egeria's opinion that his grim little affair, "The
Promised Land," is the only readable tale in *Harper's*
for April of 1894. He calls attention to a story by
Grace King printed just after his, and calls it "excellent," and so it is. Miss King's stories of Louisiana
were better, in all ways, than Cable's repetitious novels.
But close the box. It has explosive contents. No,
wait! In that blue envelope are two notes from Lamb
House, Rye. It had been hoped that Mr. James would
send some trifle to two funds for the care of artists'
children; in each case he sent orders for fifty pounds
. . . "and my little donation—may I ask so much?—
is to be permanently anonymous——" Now, shut the
box. No, shut it! Let us be reticent and generous as
the authors of the '90's weren't, when writing about
each other.

The man with such fine eyes? Egeria never knew
him. That is Richard Watson Gilder of the *Century*,
a pleasant, shy, accessible man. Egeria's riffraff of
young poets always liked him, even when he irritated
them. In 1896 he partly bought a tale from one boy
and then boggled at "the bullet had left a little blue
mark over the brown nipple." The boy protested that
the nipple was male, hence not lascivious; he even picked
up the *Century* for April and showed Mr. Gilder that
André Castaigne had unblushingly represented the
male nipple in illustrations of Allan Marquand's article
on the Olympian Games, revived that year, but Mr.
Gilder was firm, and the tale was printed in *McClure's
Magazine*. . . . Do not laugh, Faustine! There is a

certain pride and, beyond that, a certain principle in such a squabble. In 1925 the sentence, "She took one glance at her daughter's pink dampness poised on the edge of the bathtub," was stricken out of a tale printed in a magazine which, at the same time, was editorially imploring writers to be less prudish, less "hopelessly enslaved to the totems of the national respectability." Curious, too, that you may print the word "brothel" in the conservative *Saturday Evening Post*, but not in a monthly which, again, editorially resents "Mr. Lorimer's maidenly exclusion." Mr. Gilder is no more comic than many editors of this year. He had his blindnesses and his inhibitions, but one considerable merit: he liked oddities in Americana, and he realized, and said, that "it is necessary to keep this public constantly informed in history. In the United States we have a steadily increasing number of citizens anxious to be historically educated. . . . The *Century* means to keep up a supply of historical information to meet this demand. Does our attitude seem unwarranted when a public man commits such a gross error in a speech before a literary society as a reference to 'slaves contesting in the games at old Olympia'? Macaulay's eternal schoolboy knew that the contestants must be 'free sons of free sires.' . . . I think that this species of ignorance excuses Mr. Johnson and myself for making historical topics something of a specialty in the *Century*." *
So in the *Century* between 1890 and 1901 you find S.

---

* Unprinted. His correspondent had objected that Professor Marquand's article on the Olympian Games was superfluous. Since 1920 the error about slaves appearing in the games has been printed at least four times.

Weir Mitchell's historical tales "The Adventures of François" (the French Revolution seen through the eyes of a thief), "Hugh Wynne" and "The Red City," which did nobody any harm and are quite as readable to-day as novels of dolorous young women yearning in the midlands for great careers. But if you wish to know anything of Dr. Mitchell read his "Characteristics" of 1892. There is a copy in the bookcase: "To the most patient of patients, this little collection of causeries in the style of the great critic whom we both admire. . . ." They both admired Sainte-Beuve. The novel puzzled readers, and some critics, because it had no plot. He admired Sainte-Beuve, sound Burgundy, fine women and fine manners. In "Characteristics" out come his distaste for paper collars, raucous advertising, "business men" without hobbies or avocations to make them bearable, and millionaires in the stripe of Jay Gould. The neurologist's Pharaonic beard and strange, clear eyes were little seen in New York; he preferred his scholarly group in Philadelphia, where the art of dining was still understood, to the cramped fetor of New York. . . . Yes, the *Century* stuck to its historical program, and printed articles on the tune called "The Arkansas Traveller," or on the capture of the last slave ship before the Civil War, as well as William Sloane's life of Napoleon, Benjamin Ide Wheeler's study of Alexander. Paul Leicester Ford's polite papers on George Washington and Benjamin Franklin were once considered irreverent and even a little shocking. . . . It was in 1899, of course, while Ford was prudently discussing Franklin's lapine qualities, that a young author was suspended from a particular club in New York for telling the vouched anecdote of Abraham Lincoln's answer to an oratorical caller who sympathized with his labours. The President heard him through and then, in his pure, homely way, said: "Yes, I don't even get time to shave or ——" However, the anecdote belongs to what a teacher of literature has called "the manure pile of civilization." . . . So Paul Ford's mild essays on the Revolutionary great were not esteemed in some circles, on account of that lack of holy rapture which Thackeray's daughter found also lacking in William James's notes on religion. Greatness, Faustine, was greatness in the '90's. . . . Well, you'll find this historical and natural strain in the *Century*—notes of old-fashioned life in Maryland, jottings of Harry Stilwell Edwards on the Georgian farmers of his youth, a denial of the legend about the white-haired grandsire ringing a crack into the Liberty Bell on July 4, 1776, and, in the early years of the decade, matter on the slums of cities, on relief of the poor, on innumerable reforms. The fiction? Not so good. For one Chester Bailey Fernald you'll find a dozen forgotten people who dealt in a mildly moral tale of rural life or in something about a girl who wasn't sure she wanted to marry a man, and did or didn't. Of course the *Century* printed Mrs. Humphry Ward's best novel, "Sir George Tressady." Marion Crawford's "Casa Braccio" is pleasant. But the *Century's* strength was its critical side. No, the best fiction of the time is found in *Harper's* and *McClure's*. But you'll find something familiar on a page of the *Century*, in January of 1898. Read: "The maid softly put the baby into the room. She pinched him and he began to cry. 'Oh, pitiful Kwannon! Nothing?' The sword fell dully to the floor. The stream between her breasts darkened and stopped. Her head drooped slowly forward." Do not shrug, Faustine! "Madame Butterfly" was a simple, artless person before she was betrayed in Puccini's heavy music and clad in a tradition of yowling Italian tenors, and, being so simple, one wonders why the editors stuck her in the same volume with James Whitcomb Riley's agonizing "Rubáiyát of Doc Sifers," simplicity gone stale.

This "Rubáiyát" haunted everybody in the '90's. Elihu Vedder had given it a forward push by his illustrations.—Elihu Vedder? He was an excellent draughtsman of the time, much admired by Edwin Markham, Ella Wheeler Wilcox and other poets. He lived, though respectably, at Capri and is kindly remembered.—The "Rubáiyát" fairly romped in magazines and newspapers. It was imitated, apostrophized and parodied. They found some escape from the muddled aimlessness of ordinary theology in thinking that God was a good fellow and 'twould all be well, that they could take the cash and let the credit go and that the world would last a long, long time, and they might as well go to hear the Bostonians in "Robin Hood." This hedonism was involved with the rising passion for urbanity, champagne and Anna Held, beside them singing in the wilderness. People came all the way from Brooklyn to hear an imported author declaim, in Martin's restaurant:

"O Thou who man of baser earth didst make
And ev'n with paradise devised the snake,
For all the sin wherewith the face of man
Is blackened man's forgiveness give—and take——"

He would then sink on the table as though the Central Will had smitten him for his impudence, and the simple Americans were amazed. The craze increased; Elbert Hubbard printed the verses in diverse bindings of limp, soft leather. The parodists and imitators went ahead. There were "Rubáiyáts" of everything, kitchen stoves, motor cars, bicycles, and the industry increased after 1900, until Mr. Oliver Herford slew it by offering Omar's intellectual content in "The Rubáiyát of a Persian Kitten." Always lucky with his kittens, he made this one unusually good as he tucked his nose on a pane and mused on that inverted bowl they call the sky, or puzzled over the complex vagaries of his ball, the rug and the window shade. His philosophy was as sound as that of the original Persian. The flow of "Rubáiyáts" diminished, and then stopped. . . . But perhaps the craze was a nervous symptom of mental growth, a fleet glance out of so much bawling optimism at things insoluble. There was a wistfulness in verse, toward 1900; a young poet sang to your godmother:

"When all the brooks have run away,
And the sea has left its place,
And the dead earth to night and day
Turns round a stony face,

"Let other planets hold the strife
And burden now it bears,

The toil of ages, lifting life
Up those unnumbered stairs,

"Out of that death no eye has seen
To something far and high;
But underneath that stair, Faustine,
How melancholy lie

"The broken shards, the left behind,
The frustrate and unfit,
Who sought the infinite and kind,
And found the infinite. . . ."

Come along, child. Egeria is late at her concert. Shall we change this Bokhara rug into the usual flying carpet and be off to a room roofed in blue wood, above a cove in California, and sit there watching waves tangle sleepily through naked spires of rock, and hear how Clyde Fitch made thinnish epigrams in a Turkish bath? But you must not expect to be told that Fitch was a drama· tist, or even a good playwright; Americans of the '90's were not fools, my dear, and they knew that Fitch was simply clever. And you can hear, too, what Paul du Chaillu unprintably but not unkindly said of Richard Harding Davis, and what Henry Bunner unprintably and most unkindly said of editors who removed brandy flasks and garters from his tales, and how Henry James raised a small shrug, saying "I—ah—regret the malaise of transportation which . . . has detained me," meaning that his cab was slow. Or shall we slide down to Baltimore, where the cocktails will be admirable, and you can coo rhapsodically over furniture rubbed by slaves before the word "antique" was sinister, and hear how sedulous William Osler was at the deathbed of a favourite pupil? Or to Cleveland's edge, to hear how abominably Mark Hanna spoke when circumstances forced him to make speeches, and how youngsters in elder Tennessee drove out to call on Mary Murfree, lame and witty in her veranda at Murfreesboro?—She? She fooled the early '80's by writing such stiff, little, compressed stories that everybody took "Charles Egbert Craddock" for a man. Yes, several Americans were writing highly compressed short stories before Guy de Maupassant had written anything save love letters—Thomas Bailey Aldrich, Ambrose Bierce, and more—but it is always safest to accept the English verdict on the American short story, Faustine, just as it is safest to agree with nine English and American critics who copy George Moore's cheap remark about Howells imitating Henry James. . . . And in Cleveland you can hear, too, how mocking-birds raved to the moon above a long porch while Miss Ada and Miss Willie fluttered white frocks among the beaux, and the moon was inevitably the moon in Tennessee. Yes, and how grandees of New Orleans writhed when George Cable postulated that a great family in Louisiana could exist in duplicate editions, differently bound. Or shall we merely take a cab, and go up to tea in Beekman Place? These old Canadian ladies keep the poised, slow voice of their youth when they were taught to speak distinctly, and to say something when they spoke, You can hear how Frances Willard was once a jolly, human person in thundering Chicago before the Spirit moved her, and how drunken strikers were clumsily gallant to pretty women of a company playing "Lady Windermere's Fan" at Ogden in 1894, and how the players saw fires break out in the uneasy town, and troops filling the streets, in smoky dawn. Poor Faustine, you'll live so much longer in a country where nobody under the age of fifty can converse! No, dear, a girl who enters a room yelling: "For God's sake, give me a drink!" has not made an entrance, but just a noise. Or shall we build, here, a monstrous alcove blackened by all the magazines of the '90's? Pile up the *North American Reviews* and—here—take these flat *Pucks* for a footstool, and light your cigarette, Faustine.

Now you're surrounded by an amassed competence of journalism, some wit and an enormity of tiresome fiction. These are the magazines that wouldn't print Ambrose Bierce's "Killed at Resaca" or "The Occurrence at Owl Creek Bridge" because they were "grim," but brought out fathoms of verse on the Cathedral of Chartres, that lodestone of the American soul, on nymphs and fauns and Grant's Tomb, and anthems to Emile Friant, Gérôme, Vibert, Madeline Lemaire, to Neapolitan stone-cutters called sculptors in the name of international courtesy, essays on English death masks and quaint Scotch inns. Meanwhile the literary supplement of the *Detroit Free Press* risked "The Record of Badalia Herodsfoot," a forgotten weekly brought in "The Damnation of Theron Ware"; "The Red Badge of Courage" was a serial in newspapers; "The Turn of the Screw" scared people who understood it in the very new *Collier's*, and "The Market Place," refused as "cynical" by monthlies, was calmly published in the renovated *Saturday Evening Post*, as was Crane's last good tale, "The Second Generation," which not unreasonably suggested that a soldier in Cuba could have been a cowardly cad, thus alarming an editor who, in ten months, would print Henry Cabot Lodge's waspish attacks on that army. But then, this is the period in which Frank Stockton remarked that one letter of protest from some damned nobody would raise more hell in a magazine's office than ten letters of praise from intelligent people, and that remains quite true, Faustine. Yes, it was in the '90's that a power of *Scribner's*, buying a nice story about a dog, said with the composed gaiety of a stylist: "This is what happens to literature when it deserts the well-beaten track of adultery." For, Faustine, the literary republic had already created a special æsthetic of adultery. Didn't Voltaire say that marriage is the only adventure possible to cowards and does it not follow that adultery is the last pass of romance to literary republicans? True, it is the dullest amusement known to mankind but it already had its literary code, in 1896, when Charles Mason Maurice offered *Scribner's* a short novel, the tale of an adulterous couple so searingly bored after two days, in Buffalo, that they went home to their proper partners and forgot each other. But *Scribner's* literary adviser thought this "unreal and brutal," which must mean that he wanted adultery in its literary, or ideal, form, ending in repentance, forgiveness or double death, preferably by drowning. . . . No, Faustine, young writers of the '90's were aware that life and the notions of editors clashed. Some of them raged, some shrugged and put letters of rejection in drawers, where they persist, and sat at literary banquets listening to praises of "Anna Karenina" or little witticisms on the charms of "Aphrodité" uttered by men who—— Well, what of it? But, eventually, Mr. Saltus left that observation on hypocrisy wandering in the air. . . . When *Harper's*, in 1894, brought out Brander Matthews' "Vignettes of Manhattan" the general limit of sophistication permitted the American writer had been reached with the professor's gentlemanly admissions against optimism. The stories were considered slightly "French" in tone. This means that Mr. Matthews showed a pregnant woman watching her paramour's funeral and a wastrel dining with an old friend at Delmonico's, enjoying an admirable dinner, then retiring into his shadows of the street. One story, "A Summer Midnight," was praised by O. Henry in 1900, and you may see its formula worked again and again in his tales. But this was about the limit permitted the natives. . . . No, it's not an indefensible attitude, wholly, because "Whilomville Stories" and Mrs. Deland's gently Puritan "Old Chester Tales" did rouse female squeakings when they were read aloud on verandas in the susceptible midlands and suburbs. One of Henry James' unprinted letters is a tart defence of " 'Europe' " written to a lady in this alleged metropolis. There isn't the least doubt that the Americans would, and do, accept a touch of grimness or dryness from the English author when they resent it from the native. Thomas Hardy's "Tess" and "Jude the Obscure" were never so insolently and vulgarly attacked in the United States as they were in his own country. In those *Critics*, there, you can see Jeannette Gilder writing well on Hardy. They say that she had an absolute concept of the critic's duty. She resented and disliked some subjects inordinately, but when she came to write reviews of the offensive books she composed her mind and was more manly and mannerly in her appraisals than were some of the journalistic reviewers. . . . But "Vignettes of Manhattan" was the margin of sophistication allowed the natives, and at the end of the decade two writers, whose names you needn't know, gave a last shrug and walked away from letters into life "rather," says one, "than to be told to read Stevenson and Barrie, and to do likewise, when I went to lunch with X . . . and to get Emerson bunged on my nose when I tried to sell something to Y. . . ." The phrase "bunged on my nose" lacks elegance, Faustine, but immensely describes a certain editorial manner of speech. So, if you'll look through these magazines, child, you'll see a number of diverting methods by which authors escaped the necessity of removing all critical ideas from tales. Mark Twain had discovered—was it unconsciously?—in "Huckleberry Finn" that the personality of a child could be used to project realistic views and pictures of a society, and that trick begins to appear in the latter '90's, more and more. No, never use a girl as the point of projection, dear! Girls are still traditionally supposed to be idiots.

There were other modes of escape from the bloodless regimen. Romance—no, you won't find much valid romantic writing in the '90's. You'll find, in the *old Harper's Round Table*, an entirely simple story for boys by Howard Pyle, "Men of Iron," which never stops its movement from first to last. Pyle had a painter's eye for shapes and colours, and the oddest trick of jerking in some bit of mood that would be called profound psychological insight in one of the elected "great writers." Thus, his scared page, caught in the grim Lord Mackworth's garden, stands thinking that he can make a square of some pebbles at his feet with just one push of a toe, and that is the sort of thing, Faustine, that is deliriously praised in a Dostoyevsky or Conrad. One remembers a mad Negro in a tale of Virginia Boyle, screaming that the butterflies have come back as sparks dance up from a blazing cabin, and the man abandoned on the moonlit cliff in "Prisoners of Hope," staring after a canoe on the river, as the rowers sing. Buried in *St. Nicholas*, you'll find John Bennett's "Master Skylark," half artifice, half sentiment, which children followed from month to month, doting on Gaston Carew's ferocious, unmoral swagger, but not caring a rap about Master Skylark who smelled as though he'd been playing in Mrs. Frances Hodgson Burnett's nursery, until he got home-sick and became real, asking the red-haired queen, after his song had pleased her, to send him home. For the only defined sentiment that children really have, my dear, is that sense of home which, basely, begins as a love of petting not to be had on the playground and the street. Perhaps "Master Skylark" is nothing much, or here entangled with memories of grapes that nodded, as one read, blackening on whitewashed stakes, of the pennyroyal which is peculiar incense of Ohio's summer and of voices, now not heard, that called me in to supper through the flowers. No, there was not much sound romance, but a deal of that romance which is too surely an escape from decorous realities. Yes, house-holding novelists ran backward to caper among the broodmares of Henri Quatre and to dally with home life in the Parc aux Cerfs. Those rowdy French kings, you see, had achieved what Henry James called "the detached impersonality of legend" and nobody minded their nasty doings, any more than Americans minded when Mark Twain discussed that Regent of France, dear friend of Florian, Duc de Puysange, whose historian was lately singed for some realistic details of his subject's manners.

Yes, James knew that antiquity gives detachment and sterilizes much. This was demonstrated in 1896 when Petronius, Arbiter Elegantiarum, made his grand tour of the modern world, appearing languid and ironic in an ivory litter, borne on shoulders of Bithynian slaves. Wilde had crashed, the milliner of classicism, who tried in sonorous, empty poems to revoke hard contours and attitudes of the Hellenic time about which, dear, we know so comfortable little. Now came Petronius Arbiter, to whom his biographer attributed that third-rate work of fiction "Satyricon" still popular among members of societies for suppressing things, although the poet Petronius has one good line: "It was fear that first made gods on earth," a fact discovered freshly nineteen hundred years later. Petronius isn't agreeable in the first chapters of "Quo Vadis" but then you may see how the earnest Pole, who thought he was writing a moral tale, fell victim to that inner sensuous education which forbids honest men to believe in the unstable, altering fictions known as sins. Sin, said one American of the

'90's, is disloyalty to one's own beliefs and purposes, and that definition, Faustine, has its grain of sense. But his Catholic biographer bent lower and lower before the patrician, abandoning the heroine and her tiresome lover and the grey choir of Christians while he coloured Petronius, the resolute hedonist who yawns away things that he cannot believe, who boldly prefers the detached contemplation of beauty and the enjoyment of his senses to superstition and tedium. The figure cannot become real, because it is nothing but an argument and a decoration, but the oddest flutter of applause broke out in this America. Petronius was all over the place and the novel was discussed, analysed and quoted in the most virtuous circles with funny, pathetic mentions of the arbiter's death to slow music among paper blossoms. Even you, child, have seen the vogues of novels that express some hidden resentment, or longing of sensitive people, and acquire the merit of an universal mood. This Petronius seemed to be carried in his ivory litter through the market place of the image-makers and editors, and his voice came lazily in a courteous drawl through saffron curtains, saying: "I cannot care a great deal for your meritorious confections. I, who am the detachment of a final, appraising taste, have never been taken in by cheap moralities, although I have nodded to moralists whom I conceived to be men of honour and courage. . . . Yes, I like this grim poem, here, which has no buyers and hides in a trunk, of the man poisoned by idleness and self-distrust. . . . Yes, this is something! How clearly the pedlar's breath comes up in pumping bubbles through the Pacific, and how the crowds move! Neither is this image of the Chevalier of Pensieri Vanni despicable with its air of joking softly at respectabilities and its unstressed narrative grace. I like this scared recruit, wild-eyed in the battle of Chancellorsville, and I like him rather better than the hypocritical young preacher with one eye on the Irish girl who seems, Mr. Frederic, to be paste. I can be more at home in the country of pointed firs, among simple wives and old maids of a barren region, sir, than with your Catholic priests made up to show the Protestants how cheap they are, for you do not seem to see, Frederic, for all your wit and force, that both parties to your argument are a little low and that your preacher's wife will survive in the mind as the best, most human figure of your tale. I, who am detachment, am not inhumane. But I applaud your force. I can amuse myself with these rhythmic outcries against the Jew god and these epigrams in rhymeless verse, and the noise damning 'Black Riders' seems to me the voice of your nation's malady, its lack of poise in the face of novelty. . . . The poets need not press near me. What have I to do with all this twitter-twatter about Pleiades and cathedrals and persons named Omar? I am not unaware of the quiet lady in Baltimore with her definite sincerities or of John Cheney's honest sentiments and metrical clevernesses; such things are not for me, but for my fairhaired Eunice to read in her garden; her eyes dampen more easily than do mine. And your rural balladmongers make me curiously ill at ease, capering around the old swimming-hole and babbling of sin. All this stinks of enforced adolescence, and I see a mark

or so of suffering on your faces, as though chains un-
derlie your clothes. . . . Put me down, Bithynians!
. . . Gelos, bring the editors of the magazines, to
whom all these writers are mortgaged. . . . Put the litter down there, by the tall new statue of the two natures
wrestling in man. . . . Surely this is the best sculptor
of your ten years, and of the next twenty-five! Yet
I see in your prints that he is more praised because his
wrestlers have been commended among the Gauls than
for his merits as an artist. Strange, this art has not
advanced since some nameless Egyptian made the image
of the Lady Takuishit that stands in the museum at
Athens. . . . Are these the editors? Men of Athens,
I do perceive that in all things ye are too superstitious—
I beg your pardon, I was inadvertently quoting from an
acquaintance, a writer of some parts. But I see
that your superstitions are disgusting. And yet," he
drawled, rubbing verbena on his temples, "I am not
without sympathy for you, knowing that most writers
and readers of your quaint nation conceive the arts of
fiction as merest entertainment, on the easiest terms,
and that your critics constantly fall into that belief.
Will not the year 1925 be luminous with the critical
saying, 'Writers whom the great public does not take to
its heart, finally, are not good writers'? *Mehercle!*
This will be said as a covert gibe at the garrulous poet
soon to be scolded for his tale of a girl whose inner
being, Americans, seems to be unimpaired by what you
call debaucheries, and who, in that, is like a thousand
people I have known. . . .

"Your superstitions interest me, almost pathologically.

You of the *Century* and *Scribner's* load numbers with essays by Jacob Riis and Oscar Craig on the perils of the slums, and yet you shy from a stern little novel about those perils. Your essayists hint the dangers of transmitted diseases and then four of you, editorially, shiver when Ibsen's 'Ghost' is played. I have never been able to see the difference between an act of imagination which takes the form of fact, and fact. This is my pagan blindness. Most of you talk of grave and serious views of life and beg the writers to take serious views of life. But I have not time to listen to your notions of what serious views may be!

"I can praise this in your magazines: your journalistic sides are excellent. I like this article of John Corbin on the Jewish theatres of New York's East Side, these sketches of the labouring man by Wyckoff, these notes on hotels, or newspapers and businesses by Williams, Steffens and more. These, your historians will find valuable. The representation is adequate. One sees the birth of aviation in *McClure's* and jottings of the primitive shadow play in *Scribner's* and descriptions, too, of the universities where the boys who badgered Richard Harding Davis for autographs in 1890 will be yawping over 'Billy Baxter's Letters' in 1900, trash by a drummer, written for drummers. And that decline of the superior class's tastes, gentlemen, you will be attributing to the rise of cheap magazines but you will not admit that this feeble fiction which you print, these aimless tales of shadowy women and lifeless men and these tenuous 'society' dialogues have anything to do with that decline. . . . There your two natures struggle in the marble, and you do not see it! You see merely that it is best to be safe from objections of women in small towns, and meanwhile you fight among yourselves for tales of Rudyard Kipling who taunts your native writers with his primary sophistications and half ironies until three of them get astonishingly drunk at Martin's, when the Englishman is sick to death, and pray that he dies. . . . Yes, yes, I know all that! These are 'furrin goods, fotched in,' as the mountain folk say in your South, and the foreign setting excuses them to your critics! In 1922 one of your judges will be suavely complimenting an English novel which encloses a scene of a naked wench and her lover in bed, and, on the next day, insulting the native author of a small compliment to the lady of Cythera. I know all that!

"But I do not excuse you! Samuel McClure and his two expert henchmen can stand aside. You uttered bilge—I use the least offensive word in deference to Miss Gilder—bilge about improving the public taste, and then you did what you could to weaken it by inviting writers to 'see the pleasant side of things.' Your letters of advice to young artists on 'moderation' and 'pessimism' stand with your signatures! I have heard less said against McClure and his staff, and I see their hospitality to experimental writing. . . . Style, Mr. Brownell, will not always be subject to dicta of the admirable Matthew Arnold. . . . I have heard, too, McClure, your dry answer to the meddler in 1896 who protested the size of cheques given to young writers without a name. 'The boys have to eat.' That pleases me who have never believed that residence in gutters is healthy for poets. I agree with one of your few reputable critics that a taste for drawing-rooms has spoiled more poets than ever did a taste for gutters. . . . In the gutter, truly, men see things that may become shapes of free beauty, skirts that swirl, arguments of dogs and boys in love, starlights on broken glass and dung that is a jewel in the shade beside a tree. All this is not so visible from drawing-rooms, and your neat pages smelled, gentlemen, too much of orris and laces sprinkled with popular scents. I miss, in your accepted work, the ferocious movement and swift colour of the world, and the plebeian life which will remain the one thing that your nation has to give a man of taste. Who wants to be told what Robert said to Clara under gaslights of your parlours, or under the globes that will light your sons? I can like the feline pace of Howells in 'The Story of a Play' or his sketch of the Kentons, and much in 'Wheels of Chance,' where his last paragraph touches modern impressionism, but these tales have nothing to do with your superior society, and the social comedy of your time is dusty nonsense. . . . Henry Mills Alden? Oh, so that is you! Mr. Alden, in 1894 you excused yourself to a young writer for refusing two tales so mild that they appeared in *Lippincott's* without a word removed, by saying that simple folk would be shocked at their contents. So? You remember? . . . After that I find against you that you cut out the line: 'A painted girl glanced at him as he moved away,' from a printed story. It is true that you had no objection when Richard Harding Davis amiably discussed the painted women of Paris, but that, again, is the foreign scene.

And I hear of you always making little changes of homely words, such as 'breasts' and 'belly' and 'spittle' and 'sweat,' until your name gets to be rather a joke, and a source of that nervous irritation, that feeling of being treated as a naughty child, which accounts for the bawdry, the animal surcharge in letters of American writers that will stagger one or two explorers in the correspondence of your time. And then, in 1899, you write that 'our large circulation among unsophisticated people' prevents your acceptance of a story which will appear two months later in *Munsey's*. You preceded Henri Bergson in some of his philosophic contentions, and that fact has been neglected, and you wrote with taste and spirit on things Greek. Did you never notice, in those drinking-cups of the Athenian time, that the boldly elegant outlines of pensive goddesses and athletes are no less bold, and elegant, than the line that marks the satyr's subumbilical activity? You were, I hear, fond of quoting that bit about seeing life steadily and whole. Mr. Alden, your care for the susceptible, unsophisticated plebs, was it—I do not ask, Was it quite sincere? because your excuse has become classic among American editors. But was it quite—I do not wish to offend you. But, before you died, your acquaintance, Mr. Wister, gathered up his sketches from *Harper's* and mixed them in a story that is still popular among the plebs. In 1918 a surgeon tending the mashed foot of a common sergeant, wounded in your next," the patrician yawned, "holy war, saw that the fellow had 'The Virginian' beside the pillow and asked what he found in the story. 'Why,' said the unsophisticated creature, 'the plot is'—I defer to you again, Miss Gilder—'but this cowboy in the book, he's alive from the waist down.' The compliment from the lowly, Mr. Adam, seems to have been won by Mr. Wister admitting that his cowboy joked about the paternity of babies, sang rowdy songs and had seen dawn through various windows, not through a bridal veil. Perhaps the serenity of the satyr in the Greek cup, Mr. Alden, is the healthiest thing. . . . Gelos, get home to the insula and bid the fair-haired Eunice wait for me in the gardens, beside the pool rimmed in copper. Tell her to wear her thinnest gauze of Cos, and to spread moistened violets on her breasts. You must excuse the word, Mr. Alden. . . . Yes—'see life steadily and see it whole.' Perhaps another generation will have a revenge on yours for these excisions of the lifelike mention and the little word. I, who yawned when Tigellinus covered the shores of Agrippa's pond with a thousand naked women, will be bored enough with novels in which one printed ghost possesses a positive battalion of printed female ghosts. I have always preferred a selective faculty. . . . Your nation has attempted this distinction between emotions of the bridebed and those of the lupanar. But in your decade the humorous weeklies took a certain licence and were quite skittish with jokes about chorus girls and old men applauding the ballet. The chorus girl and the flirtatious woman even appeared in those humorous pages of your superior magazines, from which explorers will draw up an endless stream of sorrow and mortification in a few more years. . . . I deprecate the reputation of your nation as being one of humorists. Is not a plain

story by John Bangs, perhaps 'The Mayor's Lamps,' or
Arthur Colton's half sad 'Tobin's Monument' more
amusing than all this delirium of punning on the word
'lobster' and this meaningless huddle of dialogues between 'He' and 'She'?   I look back with more favour at
Henry Bunner, aiming little mudballs at vulgar crazes in
the pages of *Puck*, jeering at the cant of Hall Caine and
Marie Corelli, and stating his resentment of foul religious hysterias.   However, you are a nation of humorists, and the dog, as the Jews say, goes back to his
vomit.   Mr. Hapgood of *Collier's* will protest, as your
time ends, and much good that will do!   No, humorists
you are. . . .

"Why, sirs, I find myself brought down to making
compliments on the simplest that you do!   I find it
strange that your women are so much braver than your
men in dusting the myth of greatness.   How admirably
Rebecca Harding Davis speaks, here, of her meal at
Nathaniel Hawthorne's, and of her outcry when Emerson
and Alcott praised their holy war and she had to tell
them of camps fringed with shoddy merchants, ringed
with corruptions!   How delicately gay Hawthorne's
daughter is, telling of Alcott's transformation after his
Louisa began to make money!   And here is Clara
Morris, in 1899, saying kind things of John Wilkes
Booth and James Fisk. . . . And here is Aline Gorren,
in *Scribner's*, discussing French poets and foreign
manners without that lackey's respect, Mr. Burlingame,
which destroys so many of the writers who describe
European painters for your magazine, although your
service to the plastic arts is memorable. . . . Yes, I

find myself praising the simplicities of your magazines, sirs, and not their advertised splendours. I do not care for these English poets named Aldington, or is it Lang? and English novels by these Merrimans and things, in no way better than those of Nelson Page, and generally not so good. I am irreverent to essays by George McClean Harper on French writers whom he tries to put through the paces of a Sunday school, as I believe you call those assemblies of wretched children held once a week for the sake of making them loathe your God. Such unpretending stories as 'Red Rock' interest me more than criticism of Balzac written by a male schoolmarm, as I think you call them. Yes, all your magazines can find these competent tales which may be nothing permanent, but which do not make one retch—pardon, Mr. Alden—as does some of your criticism. . . .

"And in your capacities as public critics," the patrician drawled, "you were timid beyond thought. You, McClure, and you, Walker, of the *Cosmopolitan*, were more liberal to the Westerner and the radical than the rest. I, as a libertarian, caring not an as, the least of our Roman coins, for your Bryans, Altgelds and your single tax, still see the evasive fashion in which the superior magazines discussed all that. You, Godkin, will one day be regretfully censured for your parochialisms by your friend Oswald Villard. The *North American Review* was more patient in its dealings with the new movements, and kinder, than you were in the *Nation*. But this is the usual thing. I have never," he said wearily, "found much intelligent political criticism on my tours in

239

the modern world, as you call this place where nearly everything is old, and little comely. . . . Lift me, Bithynians! I have done. In short," Petronius yawned, "what you offered to your people was not a leadership but a politic conservatism, and as for the writers, what they mostly gave was a pruned mediocrity. —Yes, yes! I heard the cry out of all these leaves. Artists winced in their recovered silence. This Howells once told a dull boy at a wedding feast that writers often wrote proud stories of their lives, but that artists seldom did. Artists are men who know that they must fail. They look up from the finished page and know it is not finished, for beyond the desk is a sexless, colourless statue without eyes that does not even grin at their defeat. Then they may run to whimper on some woman's knees, or nurse their sense of bruised inadequacy as best they can. . . ."

Wake up, Faustine! The arbiter is gone. Give me a cigarette. There is Egeria's cane tapping the stairs. Straighten your hat, my dear.

FIGURES OF EARTH

It was late August of 1899 and Theodore Roosevelt, governor of New York, was concerned with a question of trousers. The burly gentleman sat, writing to a friend, and stewed the matter. He had to ride at the head of the State's militia in this parade that was coming, and there was no costume for a governor's appearance on such occasions. Well, perhaps a frock-coat and grey pantaloons made the best way out of it. It wasn't much of a dress, and the garb called for a silk hat, too. He would look a riding-master! But it couldn't be helped. . . . He sat in Albany, writing, and it may be that grossening muscles twitched around his mouth; the flat, not ugly face was already hardening into broad lines that made it, later, a writhing mask when he broke out in arguments and oratory. He had come some distance upward—or along—with a gathering strength of showmanship in store, armed with a memory that helped him over political stiles, and through his banging speeches. For, some living people say, he laughed loudly at a banquet in 1895 where John Kendrick Bangs, amusing the guests, said that "all theatrical press agents belong to a club of which Ananias is the honorary president." Whether he recalled the little witticism or not is permanently unimportant. The memory is strange: in "The Bostonians" a dozen sentences from cheap, forgotten authors whose stuff Henry James read on the beach of

Newport, and an epigram of Thomas Wentworth Higginson, appear transmuted in the slow, inimitable medium projected by that scrupulous mind. Here, then, sat Roosevelt, vexed on this question of trousers and coat, the heir of a political situation arranged quietly by Mark Hanna between sandwiches at Saint Louis in 1896. Yes, the nation had invoked capitalism to save it from oratory, and now oratory would have to be noisy, appealing to the rabble and the newspapers in its forays against capitalism. This figure in warm clay, with its female tact and childish tempers and its sense for crowds, now swells a signature across the note-paper and gives to printed record its consideration of the subject of trousers and coat in the coming parade.

The parade was first planned to pass upward along Fifth Avenue and then to wheel westward along Fifty-ninth Street. . . . Westward! . . . Odd, how all dying things turn to this West, the region of questions? So mourners on the Nile consigned the mummied citizen to the mercies of the West and soldiers of the recent muddy muss in upper France "went West" to join Hiawatha, King Arthur and the ecstatic nun Petronilla who saw God descending from the West in the shape of a fish-hook to lift her virgin soul into bliss. The great parade with its President and admiral and heroic soldiers would pass and mingle with these legends.

The whole nineteenth century had been rotten with the disease of greatness and its wretched successor seems unwilling to get rid of this malady. Greatness, to be sure, has existed ever since fear first made gods in this world and men invoked them to witness the twin vulgarities of success and failure. "To have had our little quality" isn't enough and there come the passion for a following flicker of heads that turn in the smoke of restaurants, the monthly necessity of a visit to the photographer, that willingness to flood admirers with correspondence, to be seen at banquets, to fuss a trifle about a costume in the great parade. . . . The nineteenth century had been prolific of parades and ached in its last ten years with news of them. Earthen figures sat in carriages or on horses and, granted an apex of greatness, lay in hearses and paraded while troops with reversed muskets lined gutters and sweated, being base creatures, in their uniforms. . . . A tall young Philadelphian saw much of this tinselled movement and will have, one day, a second value. He was expensively hired to tell the world about Nicholas Romanov setting the crown of Russia askew on his thick head in a torpor of incense and in such a reflected dazzle of golden cloth that Richard Harding Davis's eyes reddened. Ladies, that night in Moscow, went hunting lotions from hotel to hotel jammed with Americans, all for R. H. D. His life was spent in a hurry from show to show and names were tagged to sights: "Sarah Bernhardt"—a woman whose Empire bonnet is drawn down to her painted eyebrows, lying in a phaeton banked with white roses that glides through the flower battle in Paris. Nursemaids and virgins stare after the great courtesan with frightened admiring eyes—or, being our mother's son, we think the eyes were frightened. "Julia Ward Howe"—an old, stooping woman declaiming "The Battle Hymn of the Republic" in a drawing-room of Commonwealth Avenue, in dying Boston. "Oscar Wilde"—a tall man pent into a tight coat at luncheon in London who tries to trip him into criticizing a French painter and then sits sulking when the American is not tripped. After some years an English doctor comes to a hotel in Paris and asks if Mr. Davis can let him have a few hundred francs for Oscar Wilde "the great dramatist," and gets mauve bills stuffed in an envelope. "William Dean Howells"—a quiet, grey little man who denied genius altogether, whose talk wandered easily from the colours of Venice to the making, in primitive Ohio, of a terrible sweetmeat known as "peach leather," who, alone in the literary republic, had the courage to ask mercy for the anarchists officially murdered in Chicago. . . . His dislike of assassination was instinctive. He once stood at a reception listening while a female humorist destroyed the arts of Thomas Hardy, George Moore and Henry James and suddenly he began to tell anecdote after anecdote of his alarmed provincialism when he first came from Boston to New York. At the twentieth recital of his tremours and bewilderments, the lady bulkily withdrew her humours into another room. Her public greatness had been subtly rebuked, without a word addressed to her. "Queen Victora"—a turtle-shaped person nodding in a huge carriage down the streets of London at her Jubilee, a little figure drowsy under a parasol at Ascot in the Royal Enclosure with a tall Hindu servant constantly picking up the scarf that droops from her shoulders. . . . The gowns at Ascot seem monotonous and badly worn, and parading celebrities have a look of caged animals. Mr. Davis yawns a little. He cannot manage to be wholly taken in by this Europe, and he winces, in the land of sportsmanship, when big policemen swim out, hand over hand, in a yelling crowd at the Derby, to rescue a bookmaker, half naked and bloody, from disappointed creditors. "Carnot"—something in a black and silver catafalque with Casimir-Perier walking behind its wheels, unguarded. A stand collapses at the corner of the Rue Castiglione and Mr. Davis winces when the French soldiery scuttle from the crackling noise. Greasy papers float on the asphalt after the long funeral has passed. Mr. Henry James, otherwise delighted with "About Paris," is vexed by those greasy papers and gently scolds Davis at dinner in London. "Réjane"— an ugly, graceful woman screaming and weeping in an artist's garden when she is shown Aubrey Beardsley's poster of her face with its Cytherean grin. Mr. Davis leaves the scene in his unprinted notes and, later, tells it on a condition of silence, for Réjane is then still alive and one does not tell unkind stories about women. "Yvette Guilbert"—tall, red-haired, strolls down the stage at a daylit rehearsal at the Ambassadeurs. Other actresses smile civilly with half-closed eyes and men stir as though a whip had touched them. "William McKinley"—men link their hands and make a long aisle through the swarm of the inaugural ball in Washington. The little President goes by, with his pretty, invalid wife on his arm. "Alexandre Dumas"—a dark, small-eyed man who sits during an inane speech at the Institute, staring up at women in the gallery. Mr. Davis is impressed by the grace of manner and the air of tired reserve. . . . He has an odd feeling for manner. Is there not an ele-

ment of vulgar fraud surrounding Aristide Bruant, the
"new Villon" in his café where guests are pillaged for
copies of songs and photographs of the people's champion?   But Bruant sings:

> "Christ aux yeux doux
> Qu'es mort pour nous,
> Chauff' la terre oùs—
> Qu' on fait leur trou!
>   Pierreuses,
>   Trotteuses,
> A' marchent l'soir,
> Quand y fait noir,
>   Sur le trottoir . . ."

and he sings well.   But isn't he putting some of this on?
Other, older and more cultivated Americans will accept
Bruant at his own stated pretensions and write grave
paragraphs on him in *Scribner's* and *Harper's*.   The new
Villon will die and his greatness will have been forgotten
by journalists who write his obituaries in American newspapers.   "Franz Joseph"—a stagnant old thing in a
chair, watching the procession of Hungarian nobles in
outrageously wonderful clothes parading on Saint
Stephen's day in Buda Pesth.   "Theodore Roosevelt"—
the burly figure of earth with its blue neckerchief hurries
ahead of Davis in the hot olive woods at Las Guasimas
and stands in a prodigy of sunlight below the hills outside Santiago de Cuba, talking a good deal to reporters.
. . . Then great ladies, backing the war in South Africa,
chatter in verandas at Capetown, and the astonishing
nineteenth century ends its list of parades and conse-
quences.   Mr. Davis has not criticized its last decade,

but he has seen the greatness and parades, and they
remain, glitteringly stored in his swift, smooth sketches
and long reports.

Another tall young American had missed all the sights
and figures, although he had early seen greatness and
had even smelled it, for the dimness that picked up a
child of four from the nursery's floor in Saint Cyr
smelled of tobacco, and that is all that Charles Maurice
recalls of Gustave Flaubert. However, the smiling
"Monsieur Guy" who taught him French tennis at
Arcachon was naturally clear in his mind, and among his
multitudinous rejected manuscripts is one saying that he
thought Guy de Maupassant dull in many things.
Chicago's smoky air tormented the boy's lungs; he stood
with Stevenson's face haloed in straggling furs before
him in the lane at Saranac and eight years later saw, for
a wet second, a yellow skeleton in waterproof fighting
an umbrella on steps of a chapel in Mentone, and
recognized Aubrey Beardsley. . . . But this was his
last greatness until doctors pronounced his lungs able
to stand unselected airs and he cautiously spent a month
in Buffalo with his sister, in 1899. There was no greatness around there, but he went out to call on Elbert
Hubbard in East Aurora.

"I admit the dramatic manner and the necktie but I
must say that he seemed shrewd. He talked about a
number of people very adroitly, saying things which
have been said since their deaths by biographers and
critics of high degree. . . . Just as I was leaving he
asked me, very suddenly, what I thought of Rudyard
Kipling. There was only one attitude for a young

American in 1899 as to Kipling. Mr. Hubbard listened and then he remarked: 'I wonder what you will be thinking of him in twenty years. Come and tell me if we are both alive.' . . ."

For nine years the nigromancer's coloured shadows danced out of his pot, and literary republicans watched the parade in maddened speculation. Some of them saw this: the American public, considered a nervous virgin by its guardians, was avidly buying a fiction in which everything not permitted to the native writers was done and said openly, and gave no offence.*

Why, certainly! Rudyard Kipling wished to mention the shapelessness of a pregnant Cockney woman, howling in a street with naked breasts. It interested him to relate Love O'Women's locomotor ataxia, which, says a character in the tale, comes from being called Love O'Women, and to send the dying man back to a mistress in a brothel for the sake of a theatrical death. The subalterns flirted with married women, drank their whisky and soda, gambled and blew their brains out with

* I suggest that some historian of criticism in the United States amuse himself by comparing reviews of "The Light That Failed," to those of "McTeague," or the many discussions of "The Record of Badalia Herodsfoot" to those of "Maggie" and "George's Mother." Shifting from Kipling to the brilliant, luckless George Douglas, compare reviews of "The House with the Green Shutters" to adverse notices of "McTeague" and "George's Mother." The reader not interested in fiction must excuse this missionary foot-note. Douglas's novel is, psychologically, an act of revenge on the environment of his boyhood. He was illegitimate, the son of a maidservant in a small Scotch village and the characters of his story are fairly hated into life. The story involves debauchery, cancer, cowardice and, at the end, parricide—marred by a suggestion taken from "Oliver Twist," which was one of Douglas's books in his dreary childhood. But the story was reviewed respectfully by American critics who simply sent "George's Mother" and "McTeague" to the literary hell.

some detail in lonely bungalows. The nigromancer brought a raving shadow down to roll a dead man's head and the crown of an Himalayan empire on a journalist's table in the middle of night. Georgie Porgie's forsaken Burmese woman sobbed below his house beside the river. A drunken workman flooded the platform of an English station with his spew. Merry lads at an English school buried a cat under a floor and let its stench revenge them on a disliked master. Lalun, of the world's most ancient profession, jested with her lovers in the gay room on the city wall and had the approval of Mr. Theodore Childs, who, elsewhere, saw, regretfully, that American writers were attempting to introduce "depraved women, subjects for pity but not for literature," into the national fiction. The reporter passed through Indian slums and hauled out shadows of white women sold to the Hindu; Vice, draped in jewels, salaamed from her doorway. Salty words cropped everywhere on the verbal structure of the spreading illusion. Cheers for the sergeant's weddin'! Give 'em one cheer more. Grey gun 'orses to the lando, an' a rogue is married to an 'ore! But he talked as directly, as personally, as William Lloyd Garrison had talked to subscribers of the *Liberator* or as William Allen White was now talking to subscribers of the *Gazette*, in Emporia, Kansas. The little friend of all the world, sitting next to you on the bench in the barber's shop, was not even so impersonal as George Ade, telling of the preacher who flew his kite or the fool killer's meditation at the county fair in "Fables in Slang." This excusing presence, the speaking voice, so inaudible in the bewildering sharp anecdotes of Stephen Crane, or in the slow, grave narration of "McTeague," was at their ears. The Americans, under conduct of the sophisticated Methodist, went out for to admire and to see the world, and couldn't stop it if they tried. And then—rapture! —he told stories of America! and told them with none of that detached superciliousness of "The Bostonians," either! The millionaire's private car lunged from Los Angeles to Boston, with that quite American note of pleasure at the record made, when the trip is finished. Eugene Debs and all those unsettling characters were rebuked in "The Walking Delegate," parabolically, and force and speed were sincerely admired as Henry Adams, sardonically, reverenced the dynamo in Paris. It was too good to be true. Here was somebody willing to take the American's side against European condescension and to brag with him of machinery, and to hold the balance level, in "An Error in the Fourth Dimension," between Yankee impulse and British stolidity. He had become a national fact; before 1896 he was mentioned and quoted in, at least, five hundred tales and essays in the magazines. Criticism, or what there was of it, consented to everything, after some shiverings, and read "Captains Courageous" with the warm thrill that rises in the American author when he sees ten words of amiable patronage by a French journalist follow his name in a Parisian review of the third consideration. The mania grew; "The White Man's Burden" pleased imperialists, and then "Kim" commenced its devolution in *McClure's*. A great writer had been created. This was his longest, his most elaborately written work. Then, with a sort of

gasp, the critics, and that indefinite film of literary amateurs which exists even in America, saw that here, in the
gorgeous, infinitely piled fabrics of the legend, was just
Dick, the Boy Detective, inevitably successful from first
to last, and the illusion of ten years shredded upward.
Then anger of disappointed sentimentalists snapped into
fire: critics wheeled with the smartness of Mulvaney's
squad at drill. Amnon loathed his Tamar, and farewell
the nigromancer! But there remained the great writer,
of the '90's, and a coroner's jury of idolaters either called
the live corpse names—"cheap journalist," "press agent
of Empire," "inspired hack," and the pleasing like—or
heaped wreaths. "Ten years ago," Harris Merton Lyon
said in 1907, "they were all saying KIPLING, and now
they say, Kipling—oh, yes!"

But the nigromancer's smokes had coloured, falling
here and there on manuscript, much printed excellence.
That final literary analyst will pluck out phrase after
phrase, whole sentences and derived paragraphs from
the work of men who have shrugged Rudyard Kipling
into a remote vulgarity, that imaginary limbo from
which authors return as annoying spectres. He has his
lien on the goods of wiser writers, of men more speculative as to the awkward and insoluble; whole novels
have been spun on plots which stand, in his earlier
sketches, as outlines and anecdotes. The collapsing,
drugged measures of the dreamed adventure in "The
Brushwood Boy," have suggested long passages in modern impressionism. His delicate notices of noise have
been complacently adopted by those, the terribly superior,
who so often will take a plot or an image from anybody,

who write "A Connecticut Yankee in King Arthur's Court" for a second time in terms of William Morris plus Henry James, or tranquilly rescore the classic music of: "There are no fields of amaranth on this side of the grave; there are no voices, O Rhodope, that are not soon mute, however tuneful; there is no name, with whatever emphasis of passionate love repeated, of which the echo is not faint at last. . . ." The rhetorical address, so thoroughly criticized when Harry Leon Wilson said that King Solomon composed somewhat in the crisp style of Mr. Kipling, the directness of narrative—from him to them—and the obvious smartness of epithet were copied promptly, but the evasive, frequently beautiful statements in colour and sound have too plainly haunted sensitive artists, and the nigromancer's tacit revenge will be, simply, a record of derivations and an acknowledgment of many inventions.

He had met the unspoken, half conscious wish of Americans for an entertainment which would reverse the formulas of Louisa May Alcott. This primary sophistication admitted, by not denying, that champagne, music halls and good cigars were not evil. He had, by an accident of birth and travel, enlarged the literary map. Fans of descending vision opened from his tales; the society of Simla, an evening in Topaz, Colorado, and the marriage of a princeling in Ghokral Seetarun flashed, in temporary outline, on eyes of readers in American towns growing weekly more hideous. A plane in the world showed with one expert paragraph that displays the wives of engineers and chandlers, dependent on the safety of steamers. A massive catalogue in mere geographical reference existed, and increased with every volume of the tales. The effect, necessarily, was that of implicit romance to people whose day passed in a quarrel with the cook, a conference with the book-keeper at the office, a call from the high-school superintendent and the disintegrating excitements of six-handed euchre or a meeting of the lodge after dinner. His status as apologist of Empire, the schoolboy's patriotism and the fact, not immediately visible, that he reported but seldom analysed his tremendous cast—all those objections were worthless. They saw the spinning earth, and saw it through rigidities of a temperament that defended them; unyielding wires protected the children from the wolves. Sin, with some lenities against concepts of Dwight Moody and Francis Willard, was still sin, and God, addressed so vehemently, was clearly God.

Under the stir and chromatic rippling of the general narrative, came the claim on that "uncultivated hunger for pathetics." The pathos ranged from candid appeals to the pity of children, which is perhaps more common than affection for children, to the simplicities of a statement in misery. He had, and had in better control than any other writer of the times, a sense of the point at which an explosion of sentiment may be allowed to crash on the reader. It is singularly idle to talk, here, of his intentions, for his intentions are only to be stated by those prodigies in criticism who begin reviews by saying: "This writer means——" Who knows, pending the discovery of some admission, what Henry James intended in that last wrenched paragraph of "The Beast in the Jungle" or if he wished his audience to sympathize with the ignoble Julia Bride? There is nothing in this range of narrative comparable to "Riders to the Sea," or an understatement so mutely graceful as Jurgen, turning from his grandmother's corner of the Christian heaven. But the broken lullaby of the child-less woman in "Without Benefit of Clergy" and the lama's sudden outcry before the Gates of Learning in "Kim" remain touching, until some alteration of the human mood dismisses them to that museum whose principal exhibit is the death of Little Nell. And, even in his excesses, the journalist never committed such a thing as the last chapter of Pierre Loti's "Matelot," the literary onion, as vulgar as possible, arranged by dressing a sailor's mother in her best clothes and sending her to meet news of his death in the Orient, then invok-ing Christ and the saints to help her out of Loti's situa-tion, applauded in America and England as "irony." . . . This pathos in its variable quality was an addi-tional claim of Rudyard Kipling on his enslaved popu-lation; and in this capitalist of story-telling, the Ameri-cans of the '90's had their wish. He was, in much, themselves; but, in much, an artist of extraordinary forces, he whirled before them a vision, a gleaming newspaper whose columns enclosed anecdotes of red-coated Irishmen, tougher than those of their own fiction, mundane women, notes on ships and engines, rachitic splendours of a millionaire's private car and green country-sides in the England then dominating their per-plexed desire for some decoration. Is it absurd to guess that this reiterated, constant advertisement of the East, the thread of imperial thinking, and the unlimited suggestion of dominion over isles and forests, influenced plump men in Washington after Dewey had won his little battle in Manilla Bay and the Orient, that immense and empty mystery of all literature, had been entered by American troops?

Well, Theodore Roosevelt pondered his costume for the great parade and, after some weeks, somewhere in New York, put on a black coat, a pair of grey trousers and the other necessities of a cool morning. He dressed. Troops and admirals, presidents and senators, got themselves clad for high occasion. The city dressed itself from end to end. . . . An unimportant creature, here apologetic, was sternly removed from bed and had to think of trousers in a sleepy tangle of wonders about this parade. His consciousness began, once, when the grandfather who knew Sitting Bull lifted him and someone brushed down dust thickened on panes by those hot storms that smear windows in the valley of the Missouri with grey, baked powders. A parade wonderfully moved for him under blowing cottonwoods; striding giants of dust marched past the leaves and, below them, fans of plumage rippled, faces were scarred with streaks of green and red and squaws were blanketed lumps on the dragging slopes of travois behind ponies of the tribe. One naked little girl was an oily statue with a red rag about her stiff black hair, serene on a white horse, and an old chief rode with strings of shivering wampum and bright shells swaying on his stark ribs. The last of a great tribe moved so, glowed so, between two lines of troopers in blue coats. Covered wagons, stamped "U. S. A." in scarlet on the cloth of jolting hoods, spaced the parade. "Blackfeet, sonny. Going up to the new reservation." They passed along, endlessly to his awe, and a tanned trooper swung his horse over the low iron rails, to whirl down from one stirrup and catch up his hat blown among geraniums flattened by the wind. Then the colour of a guidon flared; a bugle yelled far up the street, and the dust closed down. "Time for little boys to be in bed." The World's Fair was a silver fish of wax on an elastic cord and it vanished, tragically, down the maw of an enormous English mastiff in Saint Paul where veils of thin colours shook at night and shed fugitive tones on the prodigiousness of snow that heaped the yard. The Northern Lights, and the sharp lights of Chicago seen sleepily through rain, join to lights of farms seen on so many nights as trains brought his bewildered unimportance from East to West, in a confusion between the tall grandfather mysteriously ruined in "the cattle war" and the other grandfather who sometimes drew little pictures on margins of fat law books or played a violin in jade dusk, crooning out "Lord Ronald" on sorcerous strings that merely yapped, when privately investigated. This unimportance lived in chronic bewilderments of aunts. Impalpable, perhaps sinister, creatures were always somewhere on the dark edge of conversations, Populists, Pierre Loti, Richard Harding Davis, Little Lord Fauntleroy, Major McKinley, Henry James and Grover Cleveland who, at least, was adequately visible in coloured cartoons of *Puck*. Boys in blue shirts ran, bawling: "Hey! Coxey's army's comin'!" once, and once, incredibly, the Missouri rose and flooded a cellar so that the more

Western grandmother stood wringing her thin hands on steps, lamenting preserves and jellies all afloat around a tub in which the neglible creature navigated, happily wet, wet as he got to be, sitting on a grand stand opposite a white, dripping thing which was Grant's Tomb, with President McKinley very miserable above the soaked procession, bending suddenly out as a horse slipped. Even the great submitted to rains of that decade. General Miles was something tall, sliding his uniform out of the moist grace of a military cloak in a hallway at West Point, not then a bastard operatic Valhalla of cement and stone.

Bewilderments multiplied, with a cold internal shrinking as the unimportance was led along tremulous floors of a train to be seen by Mr. Hanna, a person imagined as the brother of the fearful Hanno in "Salammbô" who bathed his leprosy in blood. Mr. Hanna, though, seemed placid in his stateroom with a gang of standing gentlemen, somehow suggesting amorous dogs, who watched the hands which had played on the emotionalism of a nation as though it were a piano's keyboard. The hands stopped their movement among cards on a table and the voice said anxiously: "But you've got some other children, Beer?" Relieved, he picked up his cards again, and the train came to Washington. A Mr. Hay stooped to shake hands and left an impregnable belief that he was a decent, although elderly, person. The unimportance yawned at a piece of metal shaped as a cloaked woman who was Mrs. Henry Adams, in a cemetery, and, as she was dead, very dull to consider. . . . Frances Willard was also dead. A woman came screaming into the peace of the Ohio garden: "Girls! Girls! She's gone!" The sky had fallen, somewhere! "Run down to the barns, dear. Miss Willard's dead and poor Kate was so fond of her!" The negligible identity, sure that this corpse must be in the flat town beyond the orchard, roamed between two pastures and examined empty plots in the cemetery, a very friendly one, where a mason made the sound of a marmoreal castanet, chipping lies on stones. . . . Now he had to get into his best trousers and go to the parade, and the silver morning was sharp around him; the Hudson sparkled beside the pulsing train, and earthen figures packed the streets. Long draperies of flags and streaks of restless bunting dangled before brown fronts of that Fifth Avenue. Here was the Plaza Hotel with a charming bronze lioness on a pedestal in the midst of the lobby. He had to stop looking at this glory to shake hands with Mr. Henderson, who criticized music in the *Sun*, but whose hair was different, much shorter, than that of Mr. Meltzer, who criticized music, too, and sat in Bronson Howard's veranda on Nantucket Island, consulting him about the graver arts. A long room overlooked the square, not then defaced by a high metal woman waving her stupidity at the gilded image of Sherman, and flags memorably shook above bronze cliffs of hotels on the eastern side of the street. This was Central Park, northward, and a red house like the castle in "Ivanhoe" to the south, and blue policemen shoved crowds about. The parade would happen in an hour. Meantime a pretty aunt laughed excitedly and gentlemen helped themselves to glasses filled with hissing yellow liquid from a gaudy bottle close to the huge, ormolu piano.

Somewhere down the street's thundering voices, officers were holding folk into the crossways and a victoria's horses were ordered back, back from the open space of Fifth Avenue. The curved woman in her scarf of blue feathers rose on a seat and screeched prayers to a policeman. Oh, but she must—must get across! Men recognized the goddess of the crowd and began to yell: "Let Anna get across! Let her by!" A young soldier in dirty brown khaki sprang on a step of the carriage and the crowd howled. They opened a lane for Anna Held and she crossed Fifth Avenue, laughing and blowing kisses to the herd.

The parade was coming. A flashing lady stopped strumming the piano and a rim of people swayed on the sidewalks. A bright dust of confetti, endless snakes of tinted paper began to float from hotels that watched the street. Voices of congratulation came bubbling in these rooms. Why, you could see everything from here! And this was the greatest parade since the Civil War! Greatness! . . . Brass of parading bandsmen flashed and columns wheeled, turning at the red house to the south. Balconies and windows showered down confetti, and roses were blown. The very generous dropped bottles of champagne and the paper streamers slid in facile twists and wreaths on the white and grey of uniforms. Cadets down from West Point seemed curious birds that wheeled and strode in oblong flocks. The little admiral was a blue and gold blot in a carriage. The President, and the plump senator from Ohio, and all these great were tiny images of black and flesh in the buff shells of carriages in a whirling rain of paper ribbons, flowers and flakes of the incessant confetti blown everlastingly, twinkling from high blue of the sky. How they roared! Theodore Roosevelt! The increasing yell came up from the street. A dark horse showed and slowly paced until it turned where now the gilded general stares down the silly city. A blue streamer, infinitely descending from above, curled all around his coat and he shook it from the hat that he kept lifting. Theodore Roosevelt! The figure on its charger passed, and a roar went plunging before him while the bands shocked ears and drunken soldiers straggled out of line, and these dead great, remembered with a grin, went filing by.

APPENDIX

One anecdote printed in this collection rests on a sentence in a letter of Abner McKinley to my father, dated October 4, 1896, and on a recollection of having heard Mr. McKinley discuss his interview with George Pullman. I find no suggestion in any official life of President McKinley that he sent his brother as a private ambassador to Pullman in 1894. There were such private messengers, dispatched by powerful politicians or financiers. Henry Miller, Cornelius Bliss and others tried to bring Pullman down to the safe ground of arbitration, and I see no discrepancy between President McKinley's published character and the idea of this private effort. However, Mr. Abner McKinley's daughter is alive to correct the statement if it is wrong.

On the announcement of this book a number of kind people sent me letters of literary folk of the '90's, for my use, and seemed anxious to see these treasures printed. I greatly enjoyed reading the letters, and have not printed them. Why? In the first chapter of this trivial work occurs the anecdote of Mr. Patrick Keogh's little journey in the company of Louisa May Alcott to the house of Dr. Lawrence, where he was washed, fed elaborately and given five dollars. Mr. Keogh recollects "some more women" in the female doctor's house. One of these shadows on May 3, 1888, wrote: "I wonder what became of the darling little red-haired Mick whom she adopted last winter?" Behold the literary sentimentalist at work! Miss Alcott brings a pretty Irish child into her friend's house; ergo, adoption. The same lady put on paper a version of Paul du Chaillu's tumble down the steps of the Brevoort, in Chapter 3, which belongs in the higher regions of romantic writing, and her version of Frances Willard's rebuke to Rebecca Harding Davis—she admired Miss

Willard—takes a page of note-paper to unfold itself. But Miss Willard's actual remark, as reported by two quite unliterary ladies and corrected by Mrs. Davis, was, as herein recorded, very brief.

This book, as far as possible, relies for its descriptions of literary people, on the testimony of bystanders neither inimical nor devoted to the person in question. Mr. George Warden Sims, naturally, has the most vivid recollections of Bronson Alcott's fingers digging into his small shoulder at Emerson's funeral and of Miss Alcott's outcry. Miss Alcott's opinion of "Huckleberry Finn" is taken from an unprinted letter to Frances Hedges Butler. Alcott's relation to Emerson was once cleverly discussed by William James Stillman and the opinions of Barret Wendell, Rose Hawthorne Lathrop, E. C. Towne and others were long since printed. He appears to have been one of the complacently self-deluded characters of that era. After a thorough examination of his printed remains I can see nothing original in them, and his charm, no doubt existent, must have been that "sweetness" which also hung about Donald Mitchell. I call attention to Thomas Wentworth Higginson's defensive essay, however, and by way of epitaph print one sentence of a letter from Sarah Dix, the war worker, dated January 29, 1863. ". . . Mr. Alcott was offered a post here" (in Washington) "at Mr. Emerson's instance but the latter wrote to me that Mr. A. has other projects, but I have not heard what those projects are from Miss A. or from this philosophic gentleman when he took the poor girl home in such conditions as to rouse the worst fears of her friends and their bitterest protests. . . ." Finally, I have my own recollections of hearing Thomas Bailey Aldrich in a state of reminiscence on the topic of Alcott: the pathos of Mr. Aldrich is that he did not write as he talked.

I cannot expect, for reasons of an obvious kind, that a man who was shut out of his mother's house after a wild night in his nineteenth year or another who smuggled the remains of his employer's mistress from Chicago on July 6, 1893, at a cost of five hundred dollars in fees, bribes and tips, should sign their names to public statements. The discretion of three lawyers and ten doctors has supplied me with data for which they, also, cannot be thanked, publicly, save in this ill-contrived fashion. My specific obligations to Mr. Charles Clery Nolan for the use of his autographs, Wildiana and his monstrous collections of American religious eloquence are sufficiently visible, as is my indebtedness to Grace Ralston Lewis for her notes on the World's Fair. People who recall John Wise's undervalued book, "The End of an Era," will not have forgotten his account of the cadets of the Virginia Military Institute at the battle of Newmarket and the deaths of Sergeant Cabell and Jacquelin Stanard. Curiously, a copy of "The Louisiana Swamp Doctor," one of the paperbacked satires mentioned in Chapter 3, was found in a second-hand shop in Saint Louis, in 1923, inscribed: "V. M. I. 1863, belongs to J. B. Stanard." So I have assumed that this class of fiction was commonplace in Virginia as it was in Ohio.

Reading through the proof of this book, I find myself wondering if I have opened the characters of the dead great to any malevolent insinuation. I hope not. Chester Arthur's indignant remark about his private life was made to a female writer who intruded on him at Saratoga and demanded his views on alcohol. No life of Grant mentions the several attempts toward procuring his signature to warnings against alcohol and tobacco, but the children of the avenging Titaness who stormed Mt. MacGregor vouch for the horrid performance. I don't know whether the Mrs. Walker who headed the committee that asked Dana to suppress Carmencita is the Ada Channing Walker elsewhere described. Mrs. Walker's niece was in school until 1892 and was not yet following her aunt's fantastic trail. It may be well to add that titles of books, such as "All the Brothers Were Valiant" and "Many Inventions," are used in my text without quotations on an assumption that they will be recognized. Persons interested in spiritualism need not apply to me for any news of James Huneker's interview with General Grant before the tomb on Riverside Drive and my information as to the meeting of Guy de Maupassant and Kitty Kane on the steps of Purgatory

APPENDIX

belongs in the class of conjecture along with the book of Revelations.

I am indebted, for documents and information, among the dead to Mrs. William Tod Helmuth, Caroline Secor Ames, Colonel Robert Thornburgh, U.S.M.C., Sir William Young, Richard Harding Davis, John Kendrick Bangs, Emerson Hough, James Huneker, George Walbridge Perkins, Abner McKinley, Henry Fosdick Morgan and to William Collins Beer; among the living to "Egeria," Laura Spencer MacGillivray, Adeline Gibbs Penrose, Frances Hedges Butler, Helen Kimball Slosson, Caroline Gunther, Marion Gillespie Bemis, Grace Ralston Lewis, Aline Frankau Bernstein, Helen Arthur, Ada Weber and Bird Housum, Jesse Lynch Williams, Harry Leon Wilson, Rupert Hughes, Joel Elias Spingarn, William Sumner Dennison, Charles Mason Maurice, George Warden Sims, Patrick Keogh, Amos Cliff Armstrong, Metcalf Beach, Francois Grivault, Chester Beckley and to sixteen others who, for prudential reasons, cannot be named.